Top Notes

Jane Harrison's
Rainbow's End
Study notes for Common Module:
Texts and Human Experiences 2019–2023 HSC

Bruce Pattinson

A
FIVE SENSES
PUBLICATION

T0342922

Five Senses Education Pty Ltd
2/195 Prospect Highway
Seven Hills 2147
New South Wales
Australia

Pattinson, Bruce
Top Notes – Rainbow's End
ISBN 978-1-76032-207-6

CONTENTS

TOP NOTES SERIES

This series has been created to assist HSC students of English in their understanding of set texts. Top Notes are easy to read, providing analysis of issues and discussion of important ideas contained in the texts.

Particular care has been taken to ensure that students are able to examine each text in the context of the module it has been allocated to.

Each text generally includes:

- Notes on the specific module
- Plot summary
- Character analysis
- Setting
- Thematic concerns
- Language studies
- Essay questions and a modelled response
- Other textual material
- Study practice questions
- Useful quotes

We have covered the areas we feel are important for students in their study of *Texts and Human Experiences* for their Common Module. I am sure you will find these Top Notes useful in your studies of English.

Bruce Pattinson
Series Editor

COMMON MODULE: TEXTS AND HUMAN EXPERIENCES

"It is quite possible—overwhelmingly probable, one might guess—that we will always learn more about human life and personality from novels than from scientific psychology"

NOAM CHOMSKY

What is the Common Module?

The Common Module set for the 2019–23 HSC is *Texts and Human Experiences*. It is compulsory to study this topic as prescribed by NESA and it is common to all three English courses. Remember: you will be learning how texts reveal individual and collective human experiences. There are no right or wrong answers in this module – it is about how you see and interpret material and engage with it.

In the Common Module you will be analysing one prescribed text and a range of short texts that are related to the idea of human experiences. You will analyse texts not only to investigate the ideas they present about this area but also how they convey these ideas. This means you will be looking closely at the techniques a composer uses to represent his / her messages and shape meaning. You will also be looking at relationships between texts in regard to the experiences you explore. Overall, you will become an expert on texts and the human experience—that is, the different notions people have about human experience and the various ways composers manipulate techniques to communicate their ideas about it.

Specifically you will look at one set text from the following list.

- Doerr, Anthony, *All the Light We Cannot See*
- Lohrey, Amanda, *Vertigo*
- Orwell, George, *Nineteen Eighty-Four*
- Parrett, Favel, *Past the Shallows*
- Dobson, Rosemary 'Young Girl at a Window', 'Over the Hill', 'Summer's End', 'The Conversation', 'Cock Crow', 'Amy Caroline', 'Canberra Morning'
- Slessor, Kenneth 'Wild Grapes', 'Gulliver', 'Out of Time', 'Vesper-Song of the Reverend Samuel Marsden', 'William Street', 'Beach Burial'
- Harrison, Jane, *Rainbow's End*
- Miller, Arthur, *The Crucible*
- Shakespeare, William, *The Merchant of Venice*
- Winton, Tim, *The Boy Behind the Curtain* Chapters: 'Havoc: A Life in Accidents', 'Betsy', 'Twice on Sundays', 'The Wait and the Flow', 'In the Shadow of the Hospital', 'The Demon Shark', 'Barefoot in the Temple of Art'
- Yousafzai, Malala & Lamb, Christina, *I am Malala*
- Daldry, Stephen, *Billy Elliot*
- O'Mahoney, Ivan, *Go Back to Where You Came From –* Series 1, Episodes 1, 2 and 3 and *The Response*
- Walker, Lucy, *Waste Land*

NESA has mandated that students must study a related text as part of the common module, and that this should be part of their in-school assessment. However there is NO LONGER a requirement to write about a related text in the HSC examination itself.

WHAT DOES NESA REQUIRE FOR THE COMMON MODULE?

The NESA documentation of the Common Module: Texts and Human Experiences states that students:

- deepen their understanding of how texts represent individual and collective human experiences;

- examine how texts represent human qualities and emotions associated with, or arising from, these experiences;

- appreciate, explore, interpret, analyse and evaluate the ways language is used to shape these representations in a range of texts in a variety of forms, modes and media;

- explore how texts may give insight into the anomalies, paradoxes and inconsistencies in human behaviour and motivations, inviting the responder to see the world differently, to challenge assumptions, ignite new ideas or reflect personally;

- may also consider the role of storytelling throughout time to express and reflect particular lives and cultures;

- by responding to a range of texts, further develop skills and confidence using various literary devices, language concepts, modes and media to formulate a considered response to texts;

- study one prescribed text and a range of short texts that provide rich opportunities to further explore representations of human experiences illuminated in texts;

- make increasingly informed judgements about how aspects of these texts, for example, context, purpose, structure, stylistic and grammatical features, and form shape meaning;

- select one related text and draw from personal experience to make connections between themselves, the world of the text and their wider world;

- by responding and composing throughout the module, further develop a repertoire of skills in comprehending, interpreting and analysing complex texts;

- examine how different modes and media use visual, verbal and/or digital language elements;

- communicate ideas using figurative language to express universal themes and evaluative language to make informed judgements about texts;

- further develop skills in using metalanguage, correct grammar and syntax to analyse language and express a personal perspective about a text

If this is what is required by NESA, we need to examine the concept of human experience carefully so we can adequately respond in these ways. I would recommend that you read the complete document which is on the NESA web site and can be downloaded in Word or Adobe. Understanding this document is an important step in handling the textual material within the guidelines required — remember you are reading for a purpose and should make notes and highlight ideas as you read so that you can develop these ideas later.

UNDERSTANDING THE COMMON MODULE

What are Human Experiences?

The concept of Human Experiences is at the heart of the Common Module.

Human Experiences are experiences of individuals or a group of people (eg a family, society, or nation) in life. There are a very wide range of human experiences which include but go beyond this list:

- feelings or reactions (momentary or long term): love, hate, anger, joy, fear, disgust
- key milestones or stages: birth, childhood, adulthood, marriage, divorce, death
- culture, belonging and identity
- conformity and rebellion
- innocence and guilt, justice
- freedom and repression
- education, vocation, work, sport, leisure
- attraction to a person, idea, group or cause
- opposition to an idea, cause, political system
- religious faith or belief
- extreme events such as an earthquake, avalanche, tsuanami
- regular events such as walking, eating, singing, dancing, discussing ideas.

The word *experience* seems innately connected to the human condition and it is something we have each day whether a mundane experience that is repetitive, or something new and dramatic which offers challenges and rewards. Experiences can vary greatly in their impact on individuals, groups and countries. One example might be a war that is a negative experience for a whole population while we may experience the wonder of medicine with a new vaccine for a deadly disease that saves millions of people. We need to note that the module asks for 'experiences' ...we are a combination of different experiences and each has a varying impact. One person's problem is another's challenge depending on perspective, skill set, previous experience and ability.

Experiences are widespread and often shared: this is why people tell their stories and these shared experiences form part of our cultural heritage. These experiences often inform, warn and teach across entire cultural groups and many stories are shared across cultures.

DEFINING HUMAN EXPERIENCES

Now let's attempt to define what human experiences are and shape them into a more coherent and easily understood framework so we can begin our investigation at a basic level of understanding before moving into more complex analysis and looking at how the texts illuminate our understanding of the term.

Dictionary.com defines the term **experience** as:

noun
1. a particular instance of personally encountering or undergoing something:
2. the process or fact of personally observing, encountering, or undergoing something:
3. the observing, encountering, or undergoing of things generally as they occur in the course of time:
   to learn from experience; the range of human experience.
4. knowledge or practical wisdom gained from what one has observed, encountered, or undergone, e.g. *a man of experience.*
5. *Philosophy*. the totality of the cognitions given by perception; all that is perceived, understood, and remembered.

verb
(used with object), **experienced, experiencing.**
6. to have experience of; meet with; undergo; feel, e.g. *to experience nausea.*
7. to learn by experience.

idiom
8. **experience religion**, to undergo a spiritual conversion by which one gains or regains faith in God.

Obviously there are a number of definitions according to context, but all are applicable to our study in some shape or form, as the range of human experience is so vast. The search for 'new experience' has driven much of the development of people, groups, cultures and nations over past millennia. New experiences are always met with excitement and often trepidation as to what change they might bring.

Think historically about how people have reacted to change. It can cause great upheavals in society, with violent reactions while other changes brought through various experiences are welcomed and may change how people live and comprehend the world. Experiences affect us emotionally in many cases rather than logically and when we respond emotionally, behaviours become unpredictable. This causes the paradoxes, anomalies and inconsistencies mentioned in the rubric. If we were logical beings the world would be an easier place, but probably more boring.

These definitions all point to the fact that memory is the key to experience. The experience is stored in memory and drawn upon when the circumstances are repeated or closely mimicked so we can deal with them — hopefully better than on the initial experience.

Experiences can come in many ways and the synonyms listed below for experience help us to understand the concept even further. They assist in defining how an experience can arise:

Synonyms

actions	understanding	judgment
background	wisdom	observation
contacts	acquaintances	perspicacity
involvement	actuality	practicality
know-how	caution	proofs
maturity	combat	savoir-faire
participation	doings	seasonings
patience	empiricism	sophistication
practice	evidence	strife
reality	existences	trials
sense	exposures	worldliness
skill	familiarity	forebearance
struggle	intimacy	
training	inwardness	

http://www.thesaurus.com/browse/experience?s=t

These synonyms show partly the vast array of words that our language has created around this concept, and also shows how important it is in the human psyche. We, as humans, want to experience. Now we will look at some examples of experiences and examine how they can have an impact. It is also important to remember that experiences do not have to be positive. You might experience a huge problem, a bereavement, a car accident, an unwelcome relationship or something totally bizarre that rocks your world. There can be a more opaque side to any experience that may need to be addressed.

The whole aim of this Common Module is to examine the text closely but also relate it to the concept of human experiences and decide how examining it in this way enables us to better understand both the text and the concept of humanity.

It is important that you unpack what each text you study shows you about human experiences and what ideas / themes arise from those experiences. Formulate your own ideas about the text.

Read the NESA Stage 6 document called *English Stage 6: Annotations of selected texts prescribed for the Higher School Certificate 2019-23* (see *www.educationstandards.nsw.edu.au*) for the set text you are studying. This document offers insights into the way each particular text should be examined by outlining key ideas and areas for clarification.

Human experiences and ways of experiencing vary due to individual circumstance and these experiences can change many things about individual lives, communities and the world. When we examine the concept of human experience in relation to a text, we need to examine the assumptions or biases we bring to it as well as how experiencing the text itself may change us and how we view things. The text may challenge and confront how we view the human experience or we may have preconceived ideas that make it more difficult for this to happen.

Students can also think about their own 'personal experience to make connections between themselves, the world of the text and their wider world.' Examining and enjoying any text is an experience in itself but it is what we take away from the text and apply that is the crucial aspect. That is not to say that every text will be enjoyed or offer a human experience that is significant either positively or negatively. Some texts may not personally engage you and that is fine. This is especially so when you begin to look for other related material that links to *Texts and Human Experiences*. We recommend that you find examples of texts that link but also personally appeal to you so that you can relate empathetically with them.

Individual Human Experiences

The idea of personal experiences is a popular and pervasive concept, especially in the literature of many cultures. Recording personal experiences as a means of sharing wisdom or more mundane daily tasks is part of human nature and we record and relate these experiences frequently. Experiences are recorded and relayed in many ways. We tell oral stories in both anecdotal and formal ways, we write, draw, sing and photograph our way into history (or not). Look at the proliferation of social media in this current century as people record their daily, even hourly, experiences for all to see. We record the most trivial details of our lives for likes and followers while the real world passes us by. Human experiences affect us on a daily basis and some experiences influence our lives and the way we live them.

Individuals seek out experiences in a variety of ways. Some seek more and more extreme experiences to test themselves against the world. Others limit their experiences. A lot of people prefer the familiar and don't actively seek new experiences. Individuals, it must be remembered, also see experiences in different ways and the same experience may have a very different impact on individuals. The one thing we can be certain about is that experiences are part of humanity and even the most limited of us have them. Many of these experiences also come from interaction with others and as noted we also like to share these experiences.

Experiences are what define us in many ways and are what makes us human.

We are going to look at four specific ways that experiences can influence us as people over the next few pages. These are physical, psychological, emotional and intellectual experiences and many experiences are a combination of these.

Physical Experience

The concept of a physical experience is tied into the human experience and part of the collective experience as well. Individuals seek physical experiences to test themselves against nature and other individuals often as part of trials and rituals, for example being integrated into a community. In modern times individuals have sought to test themselves with extreme sports and explorations into the harshest conditions and even space. Physical experiences can also change the way we see the world and others because of the chemical changes these experiences have on our bodies and mind. Physical experiences are often challenges and part of the experience is overcoming adversity. These physical challenges are often celebrated, as in the case of sports, but can also offer challenges if the experience is a negative one such as an accident or disease. Physical experiences are also often quite public and thus have permeated our societies in both their execution and how they are perceived. These physical experiences, even if experienced vicariously, have become popular across cultures and celebrated. Think of examples for yourself but most competitive sports offer examples.

Bruce Lee extends the concept of the physical experience into all aspects of life and that's what we will look at next in our analysis of human experiences –

'If you always put limits on everything you do, physical or anything else, it will spread into your work and into your life. There are no limits. There are only plateaus, and you must not stay there, you must go beyond them.'

Psychological Experience

The idea of a psychological experience is tied into many of the abstract ideas that people experience and can lead to a discussion of what is normal psychology. From the earliest times humans have attempted to alter their psychology through a number of experiences. On a simple level this can be a drug that changes the person's or group's perspective on reality. Examples of this might be alcohol or marijuana but cultural groups also use various substances to share group experiences. This can be seen in Native American cultures with *peyote*. In more modern times prescription drugs that are mood altering have been used to minimise the symptoms of psychiatric illnesses such as depression, and these mood altering drugs are common and legal. Others attempt to alter their psychology by seeing specialists in this area while others act out their condition leading to social and criminal issues. When discussing the human experience, psychology is a key issue and will form a part of most studies of experience. When taken too far this search for a new psychological experience can be harmful eg. an addiction.

Carl Jung, the famous psychologist, comments on the problems of addiction for human experiences, stating clearly that excess can be an issue:

"Every form of addiction is bad, no matter whether the narcotic be alcohol, morphine or idealism."

Emotional Experience

According to the psychologist, Robert Plutchik, there are eight basic emotions:

- **Fear** — feeling afraid.
- **Anger** — feeling angry. A stronger word for anger is rage.
- **Sadness** — feeling sad. Other words are sorrow, grief (a stronger feeling, for example when someone has died) or **depression** (feeling sad for a long time without any external cause). Some people think depression is a different emotion.
- **Joy** — feeling happy. Other words are happiness, gladness.
- **Disgust** — feeling something is wrong or nasty
- **Trust** — a positive emotion; admiration is stronger; **acceptance** is weaker
- **Anticipation** — in the sense of looking forward positively to something which is going to happen. **Expectation** is more neutral; **dread** is more negative.

https://simple.wikipedia.org/wiki/List_of_emotions

Emotions are the strongest drivers of human experience and form lasting aspects of any experience. Think about breaking up with someone you love and the emotions that drive behaviours in this situation. People have all sorts of extreme behaviours under the influence of emotions and these experiences are often the ones recorded and those which influence us most. Think about the role emotions play in our lives and the range of emotions from the list above. Consider how much emotions affect our life experiences, how they influence our decisions which decide our experiences and on a higher level consider how they affect the decisions which may seriously impact our experiences, such as politicians going to war.

Intellectual Experience

The concept of an intellectual experience is linked to decisions and experiences we have based on analysis and logic rather than the emotional choices referred to in the previous section. These intellectual experiences have changed the way we live and how we have seen our world. These experiences have affected the way we as humans have altered our world to suit our needs and lead to all the great advances in human society and thus experiences. Changes in our ideas, beliefs etc. alter the way we interact with the world and often these intellectual changes come at great cost.

Think of the time in Europe when the Church dominated and stopped scientific advances by calling them heresy/witchcraft. Open societies are more open to new ideas and this is what has hastened the pace of intellectual experiences as dominant ideologies fall away. Intellectual advances may not have the excitement that the other types produce but perhaps they have a more lasting impact on people, societies and the world in general. Ideas are powerful experiences and people hold beliefs strongly.

Immanuel Kant stated that:

"experience without theory is blind, but theory without experience is mere intellectual play."

Consider this statement in the light of what we have learnt about human experiences. Are they a combination of many factors or can we isolate experiences into simple forms?

What exactly is a human experience?

The titular question reminds us of the old brainteaser: "If a tree falls in a forest and no one is around to hear it, does it make a sound?"

There are two classic responses to this. The more Platonically-minded would say the tree always makes a sound when it falls in the forest. We don't have to be there to hear it; we can imagine the sound of a tree falling in the forest, based on memory of such an event or on the recording of such an event. We know that sound is just vibrating air, and it's safe to say that air always vibrates in response to a tree falling, or a bear growling, or a cicada singing, whether we are there to hear it or not.

The second answer is a more post-structuralist response: the sound doesn't occur on its own; it needs a human ear to be heard. Therefore, if there is no human in the forest to hear the tree fall, then there is no sound. This automatically implies that "experience" of anything requires the presence of a human being, which means there is no such thing as an experience that *isn't* human.

Animal rights activists – or anyone with a beloved pet – would almost certainly reject this notion because it prioritises humans and relegates all other species to a lower class of being: an attitude that most would agree has gotten the human race into an awful lot of environmental trouble over the last 200 years of industrialisation.

In his article (*What is an Experience?*), my learned colleague Paul Hartley describes experience in its most basic form, as "the perception of something else" and "ultimately information about what we have perceived." But does this make it particularly human? Dogs and cats perceive things. Insects perceive things. You could even say that plants perceive things, such as the direction from which the sun is shining. Perception is the most basic of life's survival tools for all manner of flora and fauna.

In her brief but cogent disquisition on the subject (*What is Human?*), another of my learned colleagues, Nadine Hare, asserts that to be human is a social construct. Hartley builds on that notion by suggesting that culture affects experience when we start to share it, because "the words, associations, and priorities we attach to the shared experience define how we understand the world we live in."

Hare rightly points out that this world is increasingly dominated by consumerism, which has distorted what it means to be human by excluding all of the attributes and qualities that "make people people." Calling us consumers reduces our experiences to mere transactions. It defines human experience within the narrow confines of the purchase funnel and has little interest in anything that isn't a purchase driver.

Perhaps the field of commerce is where the experiential rubber most emphatically meets the road. Unlike mere perception, commerce is a uniquely human experience. It has mediated, automated, and dominated the human agenda to the point where we are defined by what we buy and little else. Commerce has invaded the non-profit spheres of government, health, and education, imposing its own priorities and principles on these institutions in the expectation that they will behave more like businesses. And even though business still strives to appeal to the so-called masses, it prioritises the pursuit of individual wealth, and in so doing, not only inhibits the desire for shared experience but unravels the social fabric historically woven by the democratic tradition.

As if in response, that social fabric is being re-woven by our networks. As Hare asserts, "humans both produce technology and are produced through technology." Experience is shared more now than it ever has been because the experiential platform – i.e., that very human invention called the internet – is in place to facilitate it like never before, and on a global scale.

This sharing capability reintroduces all of those things that "make people people" back into the conversation – whether commercial or political. What "makes people people" is messy, unpredictable, emotional, and complex. Most of what makes us human has no place in the experiential confines of the purchase funnel, and defies any of our attempts to place it there.

The challenge for us as a species is to embrace this new capacity for sharing to keep the agendas of our hegemonic institutions – whether commercial or political – from defining what makes an experience human. A post-consumer business strategy might be one that, as Hare hopes, will "expand our view of people to include the complex and dynamic social, cultural, gendered, spiritual and racialised beings that they are." Maybe then will our shared human experience truly become, as Hartley asserts, the glue that holds us all together as human beings.

Will Novosedlik
MISC magazine

https://miscmagazine.com/what-is-a-human-experience/

This article appeared in the September 2014 edition of MISC magazine. Can you relate to what the article says about human experiences? Do human experiences depend on perception? Does the experience of anything require the presence of a human as experiencer (para 3)? Can the ideas of experience be extended to include perception by plants or animals? Hartley's idea is that "shared human experience" is "the glue that holds us all together as human beings". Is this an oversimplification?

The Impact of Human Experiences

Human experiences have impacts on many levels. On an individual level, we can have changes in our assumptions about the world and people around us; we can ingest new ideas and have these open new vistas of productivity and performance. We can also reflect and build on these experiences to ensure that they are even more meaningful to our lives. Behaviours towards others and the way we respond to the world can manifest themselves in new and different responses. An example might be that through adverse experiences we can build resilience so that the next negative experience isn't as traumatic and we accept it for what it is. Experiences also teach us new behaviours on a very physical level — if you burn yourself once on a flame you learn not to do it again (hopefully).

The impact of human experiences can also be shared in groups and societies. Firstly, let's examine some group dynamics that can be affected by human experiences. Groups share experiences and adapt and develop behaviours that impact on the group as a whole. Think about the notorious 'bonding' sessions sporting teams have that unite them in a common goal. Think about the behaviours of various gangs in our society. We see plenty of examples of this on American television where gangs based on ethnicity and social groupings form specific sets of behaviours that impact on how they interact with each other and the world. These groupings carry assumptions about how they see the world and respond to it. For example, they may have generally negative reactions to law enforcement and this is ingrained into their codes of behaviour. They are suspicious of the world and the people in it — dividing them up into threats, the law and victims. These behaviours are often reinforced by group experiences such as the initiation rituals which are integral to membership.

Often the impact of these behaviours is to perpetuate stereotypes that then categorise the individuals within these groups. The graphic I have included here shows a stereotypical gang member with the suspicious gaze, ubiquitous hoody and scruffy look. These stereotypes reject new ideas and maintain assumptions about the world, often to the detriment of their members. The experiences they have reinforce their own stereotypical way of viewing anything outside the safety of the group and the cycle continues. Of course, other groups have more positive impacts and see the world as a  very different place and their experiences are designed to be positive interactions. Think about groups such as Rotary who are constructive in the community. Other groups have specialty interests such as Animal Welfare, Surf Lifesaving and charities.

Normal social interactions impact groups and individuals, but it takes a major event to alter the behaviours of whole societies, especially so in the modern world where societies are large in scale. Earlier in human history smaller experiences could alter the behaviour of societies as they were insignificant in size compared to modern ones. We often fail to remember that many of these ancient societies' behaviours were impacted by superstition, religions and cultural habituation. The modern society as we know it is only a recent phenomenon. Just a few hundred years ago with church rule people were forced to think in a specific

way and punished for not adhering to a theological culture. Think of the Spanish Inquisition, the imprisonment of Galileo and other such restrictions on freedom of thought; scientific breakthroughs were hidden or declared witchcraft. Even recently the world has seen societies kept repressed by failed ideologies. The brutality of such regimes has left deep scars on the social psyche of nations as they try to recover. This has had an impact on the human experiences of whole populations, and societies respond accordingly.

One example might be at the conclusion of the Communist regime in East Germany when the Berlin Wall was destroyed as a visual symbol of the new-found freedom of a whole population of people who had been repressed for decades by a brutal and ever-present regime. Many citizens who had grown up in this system, where you could 'disappear' without trial or real evidence, found the idea that you could express yourself incredible. Many of the

East Germans couldn't believe that this freedom was real and that the Stasi (the secret police) were gone.

Other experiences can affect societies in extreme ways. Think about wars and the impact they have on civilian populations.

Climatic events such as earthquakes change the way that people behave and respond to situations. Catastrophic flooding occurred in the US city of New Orleans in 2005. The US President's response to help was not immediate and the national administration was severely criticised for lack of effective action.

Societies also respond to perceived problems such as pollution. In 1989 the oil tanker Exxon Valdez ran aground in Prince William Sound, Alaska with disastrous results. The effects of this event are still being experienced thirty years later.

Societies can be divided, as we saw with the election of Donald Trump in the United States of America and the reaction of the Political Left.

The impact of human experiences on societies can be quite dramatic, as we have seen, while other experiences (such as an election) can go by without a murmur from societies, no matter who wins. As a last thought before we move on you should also consider the impact of the media on societies in the modern world, and how they influence individuals, societies and the development of ideas.

Problems With Human Behaviour

So far, we have discussed the impact of human experiences on behaviour. Now we can begin to develop some more complex judgements and understandings about the impact of those experiences on human behaviours. In simplistic terms it could be assessed as:

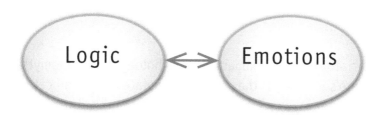

These two opposites on the continuum certainly shape the manner in which we see incidents and how they affect the experience. For instance, if someone you love has no interest in you, it creates a very different reaction to someone you don't care about having no interest in you. It is generally agreed that humans respond more strongly with emotion than they do with logic. Often, it is only through time and reflection that we can understand how an experience has changed and/or altered the manner in which we see a situation or individual.

The Role of Storytelling in Human Experiences

Storytelling has been part of the human experience since 'people' began communicating and it is a method used to convey information and experience as well as be entertaining. Earliest myths were all oral and then people began to write down stories so they weren't lost in time. From this, various theories have developed around storytelling and one is the 'monomyth', which is a template across cultures for storytelling. Let's have a look at this below.

'In narratology and comparative mythology, the monomyth, or the hero's journey, is the common template of a broad category of tales that involve a hero who goes on an adventure, and in a decisive crisis wins a victory, and then comes home changed or transformed.

The concept was introduced in *The Hero with a Thousand Faces* (1949) by Joseph Campbell, who described the basic narrative pattern as follows:

> "A hero ventures forth from the world of common day into a region of supernatural wonder: fabulous forces are there encountered and a decisive victory is won: the hero comes back from this mysterious adventure with the power to bestow boons on his fellow man."

Campbell and other scholars, such as Erich Neumann, describe narratives of Gautama Buddha, Moses, and Christ in terms of the monomyth. Critics argue that the concept is too broad or general to be of much use in comparative mythology. Others say that the hero's journey is only a part of the monomyth; the other part is a sort of different form, or colour, of the hero's journey.

https://en.wikipedia.org/wiki/Hero%27s_journey

Storytelling in History and its Purpose in Human Experience

Storytelling in oral form was accompanied by some theatrics to make the stories as entertaining as possible. Many of the early narratives were based upon religious ceremonies and stories of the creation of the earth and people(s). As time moved on, these stories were accompanied by dance, music and/or theatre and often were part of lengthy rituals, often taking days. These stories were designed to bring meaning to people's lives by explaining their own existence and the purpose/meaning of life in a time when life expectancy was short and entertainment was scarce. Of course stories were also recorded as these experiences were significant to all people and these stories run across all cultures. Before writing, stories were recorded in pictures such as cave art, in tattoo designs on skin and in designs such as rock piles and the giant carved heads of Easter Island.

Writing changed the manner in which stories were told and many of the old oral traditions were lost, barely being kept alive by specialists. Stories began to travel across cultural and national boundaries on whatever surface could be created. Papyrus, bones, pottery, skins, paper and in more modern times film, video and digital storage have changed, over time, the way in which stories of human experience have been told and shared. Content evolved from myth, fable and legend to history, personal narratives and commentary. Modern narrative form often has an educational or didactic element and can drift into propaganda. Stories of self-revelation can be instructive and give audiences the opportunity to apply learning to individual lives, whereas historically narrative was used in this way for societies and groups as a whole. In recent times narratives have become interactive and audiences can choose how the narrative unfolds.

Whatever form the story takes we all have a seemingly innate need for narratives to make sense of our lives. They either confirm our world view or alter our world view depending on the experience they convey and the experiences that we bring to the narrative. We need to remember that narratives are important to human experience and have been significant since the beginning of time.

The Text as an Experience

The concept of the text as an experience is one area to consider as we look at *Texts and Human Experiences*. Reading or viewing the text is an experience in itself and when we do this we bring our own history (experiences) to the text and this helps shape our understanding.

Think about the personal perspective that you bring to a text. What are some of your experiences that might influence how you read a particular text? Some texts, especially personal narratives of trial and tribulation or loss, can be confronting to some audiences and bring back strong opinions or emotions. Many texts attempt to do this as they convey a particular point of view about the world.

Does what you bring to the text affect what you learn from that text? We also need to delve into how the narrative experience is conveyed and how this in turn impacts upon the manner in which the story is received by audiences across different cultures. For example, Western films where heroes fight Islamic terrorism may well be viewed very differently by audiences in Western democracies and Islamic countries. Even seemingly innocuous narratives like the movie 'The Red Pill' which is about men's rights and created by a woman, has caused a polarisation of views wherever it has been shown. Strong personal experiences and viewpoints certainly bring their own understandings to texts.

Questions for Texts and Human Experiences

- Define the module in your own words.
- How are people connected by shared experiences?
- How might physical experience(s) change the way you respond to the world?
- How do you think a person's context and prior experiences shape how they perceive the world?
- Are experiences unique or do prior experiences have an impact on a current experience and way of seeing life?
- What is positive about human experiences?
- Discuss what is negative about human experiences.
- To what extent does experience shape the way we see other people and / or groups?
- Is an individual's culture part of their experience or is it something else?
- Is it possible not to have any meaningful experiences at all?
- Why do people tell stories?
- What do you think you might learn from a narrative?

STUDYING A DRAMA TEXT

The medium of any text is very important. If a text is a drama this must not be forgotten. Plays are not *read,* they are *viewed.* This means you should never refer to the "reader" but the "audience" as the respondent to the text.

The marker will want to know you are aware of the text as a play and that you have considered its effect in performance.

Remembering that a drama text is a play also means that when you are exploring how the composer represents his/her ideas you MUST discuss dramatic techniques. This applies to any response you do using a drama, irrespective of the form the response is required to be in.

Dramatic techniques are all the devices the playwright uses to represent his or her ideas. They are the elements of a drama text that are manipulated by playwrights and directors to make any drama effective on stage! You might also see them referred to as dramatic devices or theatrical techniques.

Every play uses dramatic techniques differently. Some playwrights are very specific about how they want their play performed on stage. Others like Shakespeare give virtually no directions. They might give detailed comments at the beginning of the play and / or during the script. These are usually in italics and are called *stage directions.* They are never spoken but provide a guide to the director and actors about how the play is to appear and sound when performed.

Some common dramatic techniques are shown on the diagram that follows.

DRAMATIC TECHNIQUES

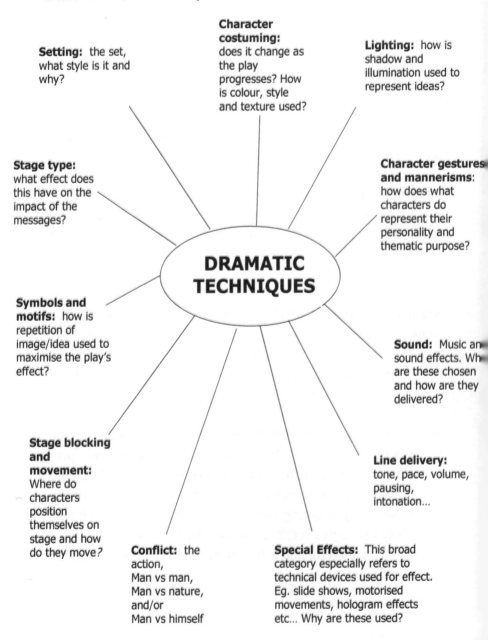

Setting: the set, what style is it and why?

Character costuming: does it change as the play progresses? How is colour, style and texture used?

Lighting: how is shadow and illumination used to represent ideas?

Stage type: what effect does this have on the impact of the messages?

Character gestures and mannerisms: how does what characters do represent their personality and thematic purpose?

Symbols and motifs: how is repetition of image/idea used to maximise the play's effect?

DRAMATIC TECHNIQUES

Sound: Music and sound effects. Wh are these chosen and how are they delivered?

Stage blocking and movement: Where do characters position themselves on stage and how do they move?

Line delivery: tone, pace, volume, pausing, intonation...

Conflict: the action, Man vs man, Man vs nature, and/or Man vs himself

Special Effects: This broad category especially refers to technical devices used for effect. Eg. slide shows, motorised movements, hologram effects etc... Why are these used?

THE PLAYWRIGHT AND THE PLAY'S DEVELOPMENT

Jane Harrison was commissioned by the Ilbijerri Aboriginal and Torres Strait Islander Theatre Co-operative to write *Rainbow's End* in 2005. A descendent of the Murawari people, Harrison's Aboriginal heritage piqued her interest in the project. Her first play, *Stolen* (1998) was a great success both critically and theatrically. It has also been on the Higher School Certificate and VCE lists for student study. Harrison honed her writing skills creating advertising campaigns and articles, and writing reviews and teen fiction. When she began to write plays she was an out of work copywriter.

Stolen's timing, just months after the Bringing Them Home Report was released, ensured that it was received by a newly educated audience, eager to learn more about the realities of the Stolen Generation. The positive reaction to the play has led to continual runs of the production and an international tour.

For *Rainbow's End* Harrison said,

> 'I decided to write about the '50s, but instead of writing about the unsung heroes...I was interested in the people who were fighting on a different level, against racism in a small country town or simply to put dinner on the table – those daily struggles.'

Much of her research came from elders who told her stories of life on the Flats. This play looks at three generations of women who are struggling with life and Aboriginality and how they coped.

Activity

Harrison has said of Rainbow's End,

> 'This is a much smaller domestic story but I hope I still manage to portray pretty big issues such as housing, indigenous people being looked down upon, those paternalistic attitudes are portrayed in the play.'

http://www.abc.net.au/message/blackarts/words/1319486.htm

As you read the play, reflect on this comment and come to some conclusions about it. Think about the human experiences the text conveys and how they are very different depending on prior experiences and cultural viewpoints. Note also the Aboriginal tradition of storytelling as part of culture and how Aboriginal people explain ancient experiences through narratives.

CONTEXT

Historical context

European settlement of Australia began on the 26th of January 1788, after the land had been declared as Terra Nullius (land belonging to no-one) by Captain James Cook.

In Western Australia, contact between Europeans and Aborigines had occurred as early as 1616, by the Dutchman Dirk Hartog, who named the land New Holland. However, the first settlement there wasn't established until 1826, when Major Edmund Lockyer was sent from Sydney to claim New Holland for the British. In 1829, Captain Fremantle sailed from Britain to establish a colony at the mouth of the Swan River.

This became a very popular settlement. Vast tracts of land were taken from Aboriginal inhabitants and granted as selections to free settlers.

The history of conflict that ensued between the two cultures was inevitable, considering the vastly different views of the land held by each. The traditional hunting and gathering routines of the Aboriginal people were disrupted. Natural resources were depleted, grasslands were fenced off, waterways polluted and the degradation and destruction of sacred sites occurred. In addition, the introduction of European diseases decimated the Aboriginal population.

The European way of life challenged the structure of traditional aboriginal society. The authority of tribal elders was broken down and more and more young Aboriginal people were attracted to white society.

During the first half of the 20th century, as part of the government's assimilation policy, it was standard practice to remove half or quarter caste Aboriginal children from their families. This practice was maintained until the 1970s.

In 1905, The Aborigines Act was passed in Western Australia. Under this act the Chief Protector became the legal guardian of every Aboriginal and part Aboriginal child under sixteen years old in the state. These sorts of laws were replicated all over Australia.

Notably, the position of Chief Protector was appointed, not elected. Mr A.O. Neville was appointed to this role between 1915 and 1940. He believed strongly that the removal of part Aboriginal people would be of considerable benefit to both them and the wider community:

> "The chief hope...of doing our human duty by the outcast is to take the children young and bring them up in a way that will establish their self-respect, make them useful units in the community and fit to live in it, according to its standards."

(A.O. Neville, *The West Australian*, 1938).

The Moore River settlement, situated just north of Perth, was a government run institution, established in 1916. It was designed to introduce Aboriginal children to Christianity and provide them with the employment, education and health facilities that western culture had to offer. Many part Aboriginal children, who were removed from their families, were taken to Moore River. It was described in 1938 as:

"a crèche, orphanage, relief depot, old men's home, home for discharged prisoners, home for expatriated savages, home for unmarried mothers, home for incurables, lost dogs' home and school for boys and girls."

In 1934, H.D.Mosley, a Perth magistrate who conducted a Royal Commission into the treatment of Aborigines referred to the settlement as "woeful". His report detailed the punishments dealt to miscreants, including fourteen days incarceration in "the boob...a small detached room made of posts driven into the ground, floor of white sand, scarcely a gleam of light, and little ventilation."

Social and Political context

The practice of forcible removal was brought fully to public attention with the release of the *Bringing Them Home* report in 1997. This report resulted in much discussion over the issue of the stolen generation. Many argue that the children were removed, not stolen, and that this removal provided them the opportunity for a better life. The issue of the stolen generation remains controversial. Overall, however, the report highlights certain facts, including:

- The removal of children from their homes was in many cases forced, not voluntary.
- The policy was aimed at breeding out Aboriginality.
- Although many did gain opportunities, equally as many were poorly treated and inadequately provided for.
- A vast number of the members of the stolen generation continue to live with the negative implications of the removal from their family.

In recent years, Australians have become better informed about the realities of the impact of European settlement on Indigenous peoples. On 13 February 2008, Kevin Rudd offered an official apology in Federal Parliament to Aboriginal Australians for past attitudes and actions against Indigenous Australians.

In view of the recommendation, by the Council for Aboriginal Reconciliation, that all Australians should have greater knowledge of Aboriginal and Torres Strait Islander history and culture, *Rainbow's End* can be viewed as an important instalment in the journey of Australian society towards reconciliation.

Some Information on the Stolen Generations

The Stolen Generations is the term used to refer to Aboriginal children who were removed from their families. The purpose of this removal was to raise these children in white families or institutions in order to assimilate them into Australian Society.

There are reports of women and children being removed from their communities to be raised in other environments as early as the mid 1800s. These indigenous people were torn from their homes and forced to adopt white Christian values and to ignore their own cultural heritage.

By the beginning of the 1900s, all states had established an Aboriginal Protection Board, and passed laws to enable the officers of the Board to remove Indigenous children from their homes. The Boards often targeted half-caste or mixed race children for removal.

In NSW the Aboriginal Protection Act of 1909 allowed the Board to take custody of any Aboriginal child if they could prove that they had been neglected. In 1915 this law was changed so that the Board had total power to remove children at their own discretion without having to prove neglect. At this time the demand for land was growing and the government moved many Aboriginal people off the land they used to live on. These newly homeless Indigenous Australians often lost their children as their homeless state was viewed as evidence of neglect.

Children who were removed by the Board were placed in foster homes, adopted or more commonly institutionalised. Many children were moved around, going to several different institutions or homes. This made it quite difficult for these children to settle into their new lives, and harder for their parents to locate or contact them.

In most cases, the children's contact with their family was severed. Letters and presents were usually not delivered to children and many children were never returned to their parents or reunited with their family. Their separation from their primary carer caused these children anxiety and distress. Many children who were institutionalised never developed bonds to their carers and never established proper relationships within the home. This lack of emotional development within these children led to long term trauma and adult problems with forming relationships. The National Inquiry into the Separation of Aboriginal and Torres Strait Islander Children from their Families found that it could also lead to self-destructive behaviour which could cause alcoholism and heart disease in their adult lives.

Government policy was based on the belief that Aboriginal children needed to be educated and assimilated. The education these children actually received was poor quality and disjointed. It often focused on training these children to be domestic servants or manual labourers.

The institutions also promoted white Christian culture and discouraged any connection with Aboriginal heritage. Aboriginal dialogue was banned in most Homes. Punishments for breaking the rules could be quite severe, the Inquiry finding that it could include starving or whipping the children.

Sexual and physical abuse of these children was alarmingly common. One in ten male and female children in institutions were reportedly abused, with the number jumping to one in three for young girls in foster homes. The problem continued when the children were considered old enough to work. Girls as young as twelve were sent out on work placement programs and many returned pregnant. It is not surprising that the traumatic youth these children suffered often led to psychological problems, emotional distress and in some cases, substance abuse in later life.

In many youths, rebellion and delinquency manifested due to their experience in the institution. The *Bringing Them Home* Report (available at *bth.humanrights.gov.au/the-report*) stated that there were strong links between crime statistics and the institutionalising of Indigenous children. This often led to prison time, again spent in an institution.

In their early teens the Stolen children were considered old enough to work. At the age of 13 or 14, depending on the state, children were apprenticed or used as manual workers or domestic servants. The wages for these workers were paid to the Aboriginal

Protection Boards of their state. This money was supposed to cover the Board's expenses, and the rest was held in trust for the worker until they were 21. However, this money was usually never recovered by the workers.

By the 1940s and 50s, the cost of institutionalising children made fostering and adoption more favourable options. However, there were not enough foster homes for all the children in care. Generally, only the lightest skinned children were placed with white families. Darker skinned children were more likely to remain in the institutions, a sharp reminder of the racism that pervaded these institutions.

In 1968 the care of Indigenous children was transferred to the Commonwealth government and a year later the Aboriginal Welfare Board was abolished. From the mid 70s, Indigenous workers began being involved in the process of placing children. It was not until the late 70s that cases of neglect and hence removal of Aboriginal children started to fall. By 1987, government policy decreed that any Aboriginal child removed from their primary carer should be placed with an Indigenous family if possible.

Many Australians were ignorant about the extent and effects of the Stolen Generation until the National Inquiry into the Separation of Aboriginal and Torres Strait Islander Children from their Families was held. This Inquiry released a report on 26th of May 1997 titled 'Bringing Them Home'. The publication of this report alerted many Australians to the terrible realities that the policies and institutions of the Stolen Generation had caused. National Sorry Day, one year later, saw approximately 250 000 people walk across the Sydney Harbour Bridge to apologise for the government policies and institutions that had caused such trauma in the Aboriginal Community.

* This information was taken from *bth.humanrights.gov.au*. Visit *bth.humanrights.gov.au/our-stories* to view the testimonies of the real Stolen children.

Thanks to Kirsten Oakley.

PLOT OUTLINE

The Play begins with *Que Sera, Sera*

In "aftermath' Nan Dear and Gladys are cleaning up after the flood

The Queen's visit is a focal point and we learn about the family

First dream sequence when Gladys meets the Queen

Gladys doesn't see the Queen as the view is blocked by hessian.

Pick-a-Box is on and we learn how smart Gladys is

Second dream sequence where Gladys wins prizes on Pick -a- Box

Dolly heads to the river as Nan points out some realities to Gladys

Dolly meets Errol and they are attracted to each other

Errol is an encyclopaedia salesman

He interests Gladys

Another dream sequence where Dolly graduates from university

We learn Gladys can't read

Errol leaves her a card

Errol and Dolly talk

Dolly rescues his bicycle
from the local kids

Nan Dear warns Dolly
about 'bad' men

Dolly gets lino from the
tip and we get the next
dream sequence

Errol is back and goes to
meet Dolly

Dolly is embarrassed
by her can cup

Gladys is working
extra at the cannery
to get money for the
encyclopedia

Gladys arrives with an
old bookcase from
the tip but Dolly is
embarrassed

Nan tells Gladys not
to give Dolly ideas

Dolly and Errol are
now more 'mature' as
Gladys gets the first
volume

Errol and Dolly agree
to go to the dance

The Inspector
comes. He talks of
assimilation

We learn Gladys was
taken away as a child

Nan pretends to be
sick to stop Dolly
going to the dance

The inspector takes
away Ester's kids

Dolly is allowed to go to the Ball

Gladys now has up to Volume K

Errol has arranged with Gladys to meet Dolly at the ball

Gladys meets the bank manager

At the ball things go well for a while

Dolly is embarrassed and runs out and into cousin Leon

Leon thumps Errol

Errol and Dolly meet by the river and she rejects him

She is then raped by Leon and falls pregnant

They move to the new housing at Rumbalara

Errol helps Gladys to read and she invites him to Melbourne

Dolly has a baby, Regina

At the meeting in Melbourne Gladys gives the petition and Nan softens about Errol

Errol and Dolly get together

SUMMARY WITH COMMENTARY

OVERVIEW

The play has four main characters;

- Nan Dear – grandmother of Dolly and Gladys' mum.
- Gladys – mother of Dolly, daughter of Nan
- Dolly – Gladys' 17 or 18 year-old- daughter
- Errol Fisher – white encyclopaedia salesman in his 20s

The 'actor playing Errol' plays other characters in the play.

The play is set in 1954 and a clear indication of conditions for Aboriginal people can be found in the context section of these notes. Note that though they live in a humpy near the riverbank they are portrayed with dignity. This is a scene from the reality of Aboriginal lives and has been paralleled with an Aboriginal community, Rumbalara (Rainbow's End) also known as the 'Flats' on the Goulburn River in Victoria.

This play was also commissioned for the Ilbijerra Aboriginal and Torres Strait Islander Theatre Co-operative. It premiered at the Sydney Myer Amphitheatre at the Melbourne Museum and was directed by Wesley Enoch.

ACT ONE

Scene One

Prologue: Aftermath

Aftermath means 'the resultant condition after a catastrophe' and so this negative notion initiates the drama, reinforced by the song 'Que Sera, Sera' with its line 'Whatever will be, will be'. This seems to portray the Aboriginal situation in the play and typifies the situation of the three women.

The playwright's notes show that Nan Dear and Gladys are 'rebuilding' their humpy after a flood. The scene is of a 'devastated' place but Nan and Gladys continue to rebuild, even using Dolly's magazines to cover the walls. Dolly comes home from school and is unhappy with proceedings but Gladys says 'It'll be alright'. Nan gives Dolly a hug as the lights go down.

Questions

- Why does Harrison use 'Que Sera, Sera' as the play's opening moment?
- How are Nan and Gladys reacting to the flood?
- Why does Dolly say 'You always say that' to Gladys?
- Look up the word 'stoic'. Does this apply to the women?

ACT ONE

Scene One (A): The Queen's Visit

It is morning and Gladys is dressing while listening to the voice of the Queen on the radio. Dolly is studying. The Queen's message fades and Gladys asks Nan where her white gloves are. They argue over Gladys going to town to see the Queen instead of picking beans. Dolly is making a 'family tree', which lists all her family members except cousins. Nan reckons you need to know your cousins so you don't marry them. Gladys says royalty marry cousins but Nan says 'No good'll come of it'.

Nan is 'incredulous' that Gladys has ordered a taxi so her shoes don't get dirty for the visit to town. Dolly learns for her tree that Nan was born on the 'Murray River'. She tells how they were forced to leave 'Cummeragunja. Our home.' As Gladys leaves, Dolly says she looks 'Fit for a Queen'.

Harrison now introduces a dream sequence where Gladys is hugged by the Queen. Back in reality she is holding a 'bunch of weeds'. Nan says she's going to work and sends Dolly off to school with a warning to stay away from the cork trees. As the scene ends, the 'lights indicate a time change'.

Questions

- Why does the Queen fascinate Gladys?
- What do we learn about Nan Dear in this scene?
- What indications through language are there that the women know each other very well? Think about how close they are and how they know each other's habits and mannerisms. Give specific examples.

ACT ONE

Scene One (B)

The radio is describing the Queen's visit to Shepparton but Gladys has seen a different picture after the taxi doesn't arrive and she has to walk all the way to town. This is also because hessian has been put up along the road to hide the humpies from the road. Nan doesn't get 'het up' over it and says it is Papa Dear's mission to get advances for the Aboriginal people. He had a meeting with the Queen. Gladys admits she never even got to see the Queen and Nan wonders where she her 'highfalutin' ideas come from. Ironically, the announcer says the 'royal couple' were shown a boomerang to remind them they were in Australia.

Questions

- What social issues are raised in this scene?
- Why do you think Harrison doesn't include Papa Dear in the play here?
- Where do we get the impression the Aborigines belong? How is their exclusion from mainstream society shown?

Act One

Scene Two (A): Oh Errol

Again Harrison uses the radio to begin the scene, so as Gladys chops wood, the Bob Dyer quiz show 'Pick-a-Box' is heard. This is a very famous, long running Australian show and Gladys is answering the quiz questions and getting the answers correct. Nan is unhappy with her listening and turns the station over as Dolly comes home. Dolly suggests Gladys enter and turns the radio back but Nan says they won't have 'blacks'. Dolly says they couldn't tell.

Nan's glare encourages Dolly to turn the radio off and we begin to see their different perspectives on life and how life is constantly evolving. Harrison again uses a dream sequence and Gladys is presented as a Pick-a-Box contestant. She has won two prizes and when they come back to reality, Dolly tells Nan to 'Get with the times'. Nan asks her about talking to Leon Arnold. Dolly says she isn't going to marry him as he's a cousin and Gladys says she won't marry until she's finished her education and gotten a good job. Note in this sequence how the interchange of dialogue between the three shows how close they are and the dialogue is interwoven like their lives.

Dolly goes to the river pushing a pram and Nan and Gladys argue over putting 'ideas' into Dolly's head. Nan is more pragmatic and talks of how Ester's got a black-eye and a baby from her 'whitefella' husband. She leaves to visit her with a rabbit.

Questions

- Research both Bob Dyer and Jack Davey. What impact did they have on Australian culture? Why would Harrison use them in this play?
- In this scene how do we see Nan Dear's more pragmatic approach to life? How does she acknowledge – and we see – what social grouping she belongs to?
- Why and how does Harrison use the dream sequence to make a point? Think about how these sequences might be portrayed on stage.
- Do you agree with Gladys that Dolly, 'needs to know the world is bigger than just this'?

ACT ONE

Scene Two (B)

As the lights come up, the audience sees Dolly pushing the pram she left with in the last scene while Errol enters riding a bicycle. He nearly falls off on seeing her and says good morning politely to her. As they pass each other they eye each other off and there is 'an instant spark of attraction' between them. He heads towards Gladys and the humpy with a big heavy book in his hand. Note here the paucity of dialogue meaning that the physical attraction needs to be portrayed carefully as it is crucial to the further development of the play and the concept of belonging.

He tells Gladys his name is Errol Fisher and tries to interest her in the 'most famous of tomes' but Dolly returns and he drops the book. Dolly says 'They're not for the likes of us' but Gladys stops him leaving and tells him to continue with his spiel on the Encyclopaedia Britannica. They begin a conversation that turns to Dolly and as he continues his spiel we see another dream sequence where Gladys sees Dolly as a graduate.

As it fades Nan returns and thinks Errol's from the 'Welfare'. He seems to have sold Gladys the set but Nan says to ask him what it says about the Aborigines. He goes to give Gladys a pen and the form but it is obvious she can't write. Nan saves her by saying her glasses are broken. Dolly then tells Errol how he has misread the map and the 'toffs' live on the other side of town. She tells Errol he shouldn't be at the blackfella housing. Errol agrees to leave and as always is very polite. He leaves a card for Gladys. Dolly and Errol set off and Gladys and Nan argue about Errol and Gladys' ideas.

The spotlight then falls on Errol and Dolly who are talking as they walk. He isn't a great salesman and hasn't yet sold a set. This trip to Mooroopna is the furthest he had been from Melbourne and she wonders what it is like. He says that he made a mistake coming to the Flats but says 'all's well that ends well' and asks if she will be here in four weeks when he does deliveries. Dolly rescues his bicycle from the local kids and he thanks her.

Back at the humpy the three women talk and Nan Dear warns Dolly about 'bad' men and tells her to do her homework. Dolly says she needs an 'encyclops' to do it and Nan chases her around with a wooden spoon. Gladys puts Errol's card down the front of her dress as the lights fade on the scene.

Questions

- Think about the scene where Dolly meets Errol. How would you have the actors perform it? You could draw up a staging diagram and block it in.

- Why is Gladys interested in buying an encyclopaedia?
- Discuss how Errol is portrayed in this scene.
- Why is Nan cynical about Errol and his encyclopaedias?
- What tells us in this scene that the Aborigines belong in a different part of town to the whitefellas?

ACT ONE

Scene Three: Lino

Dolly is rummaging at the tip when the lights move into a dream sequence mode and Dolly dreams of being served and getting her lino from a 'well groomed salesman'. Back in reality she puts the tip lino on her shoulder and heads home. On the way she is going past the cork trees when her 'cuz' Leon invites her over for a party. She politely says no and meets Nan who questions her about going past the cork trees. Dolly says the 'goomees' are harmless. Nan tells her they have had hard times but 'they're still our people'.

Back at the humpy Dolly finds Errol waiting outside and he asks her a lot of questions. Dolly won't let him inside saying there's a sleeping baby but she gives him a glass of water. He notices the cup is made out of a tin and she is embarrassed. She has a ride on his bike and they start to talk. She says she'll work at the cannery after school and he tells her there is plenty of work in the city. He tells her she could 'do anything'. She ponders job options aloud but Gladys returns with 'a crappy old bookcase'. Gladys says she got it at the tip and an embarrassed Dolly goes inside. An equally embarrassed Errol says the bookcase just needs some paint, which Gladys immediately pulls out from the old pram she pushed the bookcase home in. The scene ends with laughter at this.

Questions

- What does Dolly's dream sequence show the audience?
- How do you see the section with Leon at the cork trees?
- Why does Nan tell her the 'goomees' are 'still our people'?
- Errol and Dolly's relationship is developing. Do you think Errol is naïve in thinking he can have a relationship with an Aboriginal girl?
- What different experiences do they have? Discuss how a shared experience can bring people together.
- Why is it important the scene ends in laughter?

ACT ONE

Scene Four: House at Biba

It is dinner and the women are having stew while discussing Papa Dear when a light change signals another dream sequence and he enters. Only Gladys notices him. The scene continues and Dolly says she may go for a job at Trevak's but Nan says it won't happen and sends her for a 'cardie'. Nan tells Gladys that they won't give an Aboriginal girl from the Flats a job. An ad for the whitener detergent Ajax ends the scene and Nan reinforces her point.

Questions

- Why do you think Gladys is the only one to see Papa Dear?
- Are Dolly and Gladys right to dream or naïve? Does Nan's realism deter them? What is Harrison saying with these differing views?
- Why does Harrison use the term 'elves' in this scene?

ACT ONE

Scene Five: The Delivery

The scene begins inside the humpy and Dolly and Errol *'look slightly more mature'*. The playwright's notes indicate that Dolly is *'really embarrassed'* Errol is inside but Errol seems not to notice. They are inside because it is wet outside and Errol is delivering the first encyclopaedia. He is offered a 'cuppa' but they have to send for coffee. Gladys is getting the money for 'Volume A' from jam tins. She tells the story of picking fruit and the carpet snake. Errol's ignorance of the bush is shown. She gives him the signed contract and the money and he gives her the volume which takes pride of place in the centre of the bookshelf. She says they'll be seeing a bit more of each other and Dolly is again embarrassed. The lights fade and come straight back with Dolly and Errol outside.

They are talking and he learns her name is Dolores. They talk about where she lives and he eventually asks her to a dance in Shepparton. Dolly warns him of the problems he will face with an Aboriginal. They dance the jitterbug but *'Dolly knows their relationship cannot work'*. Eventually she agrees to meet him at the hall and all is 'swell'. Nan appears and the mood is broken. She tells him to move on 'past the cork trees'.

Questions

- How do we know that Gladys has struggled hard to raise the money for the encyclopaedia?
- How do we see Errol's ignorance of the Aboriginal position in society?
- Why does Dolly know 'their relationship cannot work'?
- Do you think they can ever belong together?

ACT ONE

Scene Six: The Inspection

Nan and Gladys are anxious, as the Inspector has come. He asks them questions about the family and they also talk about the living conditions. Dolly comes in and he is pleased she is doing her 'Leaving Certificate' and asks about her ambitions. He talks about his report and how it must change things like the sanitation. He talks at length about assimilation and how they need to organise themselves. He has tea and damper before leaving when Gladys says to him 'Do come again'.

Nan is *'disgusted'* and Dolly wants to know who he was. Nan leaves through *'anxiety'*. Nan is worried they will 'take' Dolly like they did Gladys but Gladys wants to know what he was writing about them. Nan says her ideas are all daydreams but Gladys says they are 'not really daydreams'.

Questions

- What is the role of the Inspector? How realistic is this scene from your understanding of the context of white/black relations in the 1950s?
- Why is Nan Dear really anxious? Is this anxiety justified?
- How does Harrison end this scene on a positive note? How might this experience have affected Aboriginal people?

Act One

Scene Seven: The Turn

Gladys is going out to the housing fundraiser and Nan tells her not to get 'too clever' as she will get 'knocked down'. They are trying to get housing at Rumbalara (Rainbow's End). Dolly enters and is 'A vision' looking 'beautiful' for the dance with Errol. Nan is not happy when she learns Dolly is going to the dance and not the fundraiser. Nan has a coughing fit and Dolly has to choose to stay with her as her lift to town departs. Nan instantly gets better and Dolly is disappointed but resigned as the lights go down.

Questions

- Why does Nan Dear tell Gladys, 'You get knocked down when you get too clever'?
- What reasons would Nan have for stopping Dolly going to the dance? How do we see her manipulative side manifested?
- Nan decides to go to the concert where Dolly might meet a nice Aboriginal boy. Why would she encourage Dolly in this?
- Is Nan using her worldly experience here?

Act One

Scene Eight: Washing Day Blues

Nan is hanging out the washing when Dolly comes home. Dolly tells her that three of the boys weren't at school because of the Inspector. She also says that Aunty Ester is down at the cork trees drinking with the goomees. A radio ad comes on for the Miss Mooroopna- Shepparton Ball when Gladys comes home saying there's a trainee program at the bank in town. Dolly and Nan are negative about it. Gladys responds she just wants what any mother wants for her daughter.

Dolly asks why they don't have a 'normal life' and they discuss fighting for things to get better. Nan mentions the ball and gives in, saying Dolly can go. Dolly wants to enter the competition and Nan even promises to make her a dress. Nan then tells her to 'git'.

Questions

- What has happened to Ester's children?
- Why does Gladys want Dolly to go for the traineeship?
- Do you agree with Dolly's line 'how come there's no answers'?
- Why does Nan relent and let Dolly go to the ball? What does she fear the experience might do to Dolly?

ACT ONE

Scene Nine: Home Sweet Home

In the humpy Gladys is emptying mousetraps as the cold weather has driven mice into the house. Gladys is now up to 'K' with her encyclopaedias. Dolly asks whether Errol enquired after her and Gladys tells her he will be at the dance. He has asked if Dolly will meet him. Gladys is annoyed that Nan has already told her she can go. They fight and Dolly says she's the one who gets the snide remarks and stones thrown at her. Gladys tells her they all get it and she must not be ashamed. Nan enters and Gladys takes her frustration out on her, saying Dolly is going with Errol.

Questions

- What is the cause of conflict in this scene?

- Discuss what Gladys means when she says, 'You have to learn to not let them shame you'?
- What does this scene expose about the experience of being Aboriginal in Australian society in the 1950s?

ACT ONE

Scene Ten: The Bank vs Mrs Banks

Gladys is in the bank manager's office and he asks her how he can help. She says she wants Dolly to apply for the teller position and tells him about her good grades. In the background, we see Dolly, behind gauze, picking fruit and singing 'Catch a Falling Star'. The manager pours himself tea, ignoring Gladys. He isn't sure Dolly would fit in but Gladys is adamant and overcomes his every objection, through *'gritted teeth'*. He tries to fob her off but Dolly's voice in the background says, 'Have you learnt not to be shamed by them? Eh?' The manager eventually softens and even fills out the form for Gladys when he realises she can't write.

Questions

- How is the manager's patronising attitude displayed? What kind of experience must this have been for Gladys? Why might the bank manager also be uncomfortable with the experience?
- Discuss the end of the scene. What point does Harrison make by portraying events in this way?

ACT ONE

Scene Eleven: The Ball

The sound of a big band is heard and Errol and Dolly are dancing. Dolly thinks everyone is looking at them and Errol says it is because she is the 'prettiest' girl there. Errol goes to get punch and a dream sequence shows Dolly winning the competition but back in reality it is Nancy Woolthorpe who tells us in a voice over that Dolly's dress is made form curtain material her mother discarded at the tip. Dolly runs out and a slurring voice offstage calls her over. It is Leon, her cousin, who says she needs to be taught a lesson. When Errol comes out, Leon thumps Errol. Dolly runs off and Errol calls after her to no avail.

Questions

- Why does Dolly notice the stares and not Errol?
- How is Dolly humiliated?
- Discuss why Leon thinks she needs to be taught a lesson.
- Describe how Errol appears to the audience in this scene.

ACT ONE

Scene Twelve: Storm Brewing

Gladys says Dolly will be having a lovely time but Nan has a sense of foreboding. She goes outside with a lamp and calls for Dolly, but the lamp blows out.

Questions

- How does this scene show the difference between the two women, Nan Dear and Gladys?

ACT ONE

Scene Thirteen: Waters Rising

Dolly is sobbing by the river, and when Errol comes to see her she raises her fists to defend herself. He tries to cheer her up and she sees his black eye. Dolly gets some jelly out of the river to help it and he sees her torn dress. The river's rising when he tells her she is his Miss Mooroopna-Shepparton. She tells him she learnt to punch from her thirty 'big brothers'. He thinks her Christmas tree must be huge in her house and she tells him they have no tree but a lot of fun.

They swap stories about their families and Errol thanks her for rescuing him. He shows his naivety by not knowing what a 'gin jockey' is. They nearly kiss but Dolly tells him it can't work. He tells her he wants to take her away to the city and get married. He tells her she would have a 'better life' and a 'real home'. She becomes indignant and tells him he assumes his world is better. She leaves him because he doesn't respect her and refuses to let him walk her home. The last voice in the scene is her cousin's and he just says he's caught up with her.

Questions

- How do we see the closeness of the relationship between Dolly and Errol?
- Errol has misunderstood Dolly and her situation. How does Harrison convey this?
- Is Dolly right to leave him? Is this a response to her personal experience or the experience of her cultural group experiences, or both?

ACT ONE

Scene Fourteen: The Flood

Nan and Gladys are moving their household belongings before the flood. They are both worried about Dolly. A policeman comes to help them move but they think it is about Dolly. They want to save the Singer sewing machine and the encyclopaedias but he says his orders are people leave first. A noise that Gladys says is like a 'banshee wailing' is heard and Dolly appears in a flash of lightening. Dolly pushes Nan aside and tries to get into the humpy but the policeman tries to stop her. Dolly tells him not to touch her and Gladys tells him to go and help another family. Gladys asks Dolly what's wrong but she just 'stands there helpless' and *'wails like a banshee'*. The scene ends in darkness as the *'waters rise'*.

Questions

- Why are Gladys and Nan worried about Dolly?
- What concerns does the policeman raise?
- Describe what you think has happened to Dolly? Discuss how you might perform the end of the scene on stage.

ACT TWO

Scene One: After the Flood

The flood is over but it has left its devastation. Dolly is still in the same dress and still *'shell-shocked'*. Nan sees Gladys' encyclopaedias are ruined but Gladys says that people are more important than things. They talk about moving to Rumbalara and also whether they should tell anyone about what has happened but decide it's women's business. Errol arrives to beg forgiveness but he looks at Dolly and asks 'what happened-?' Gladys reaches for the axe and they drive him off. Dolly says simply, 'It wasn't him' and the others are in shock. The scene ends with the *'sound of bulldozers'*.

Questions

- Why doesn't Gladys care about her encyclopaedias?
- When Errol comes, why do they assume it was he who raped Dolly?
- Harrison describes him as 'devastated'. Why would she use this term?
- Describe what effect Dolly's statement 'It wasn't him' has not only on Gladys and Nan Dear but also on an audience.

ACT TWO

Scene Two: The Move to Rumbalara

The radio tells how the Aborigines are moving into pre-fabricated housing and Nan coughs whenever she is in the house. They are not 'lovable' homes, but Nan says she'll make curtains.

Questions

- Why are the houses described as 'concrete, small, white and featureless? How disparate are the homes from their cultural heritage?
- How does this description differ from the views of the radio announcer?

Act Two

Scene Three: The Broadcast

On the radio is a man playing a gumleaf and Dolly and Gladys argue about the interview at the bank. She changes the station to a broadcast about Aboriginal Housing at the Council. Dolly tells her to 'fix her own house' and Gladys says she will as she exits. Nan talks to Dolly but the rent man, Mr Coody, interrupts as Nan pays him the rent. She joins Dolly in shelling peas. Dolly says Nan never reads but Nan whispers she can't in front of Gladys. Suddenly on the radio they hear Gladys at the council meeting and she continues to interrupt until she is elected. Before she goes she tells them, 'this is my land' and that she has only just started on 'the housing problem'. Nan swears in German when the valve goes and Dolly is shocked. They are both proud of Gladys.

Questions
- Why can't Dolly realistically go for the job at the bank?
- Why does Gladys leave? Summarise what she tries to say at the meeting
- Discuss why Harrison ends the scene with the jig.

Act Two

Scene Four: The Contract

Errol comes up to the new house and Gladys lets him approach. He tells her she needs to write a letter to cancel the contract and they do it together. She says she is sorry that he was treated unfairly and she asks him to teach her how to write. He agrees but she reminds him Dolly won't see him. He says he will prove he's 'worthy of her' and she encourages him.

Questions

- Why has Errol come back?
- List what we learn about Gladys' life.
- How is Errol portrayed in this scene?

ACT TWO

Scene Five: Pay the Rent

'Somewhere Over the Rainbow' plays and Nan is cooking outside. The rent man tells her that the house is not 'suitable for an extended family'. He treats Nan badly and bossily and raises her ire. She ends up throwing eggs at him. Dolly is surprised by her anger but Nan only sees how *'vulnerable'* Dolly looks. Dolly tells Nan she is worried she won't love the child because of how it was conceived but Nan says the child will be loved anyway. Nan tells Dolly of how Gladys was the product of her union with a whitefella before she married Papa Dear. That is one reason she tried to stop Dolly seeing Errol.

Dolly tells Nan that Errol wanted to take her away and marry her. Nan says you have to leave the things you love behind sometimes, but says she can't marry Errol because the whitefella she was with was Clem Fisher and might be related to Errol. Dolly says she likes Errol but will give him up for Nan's sake. They agree to keep their secrets, Nan tells her 'Everything'll be fine' and the scene ends with them together.

Questions

- How is the rent man portrayed?
- List what we learn about Nan Dear in this scene.
- Do you think 'Everything'll be fine' in the end? Explain your answer.

Act Two

Scene Six: Errol Spills the Beans

Gladys and Errol are sitting on a park bench and they are discussing the council meeting and her 'radio moment'. He is helping her read the Inspector's report. She is learning well but gets nervous in front of people. They talk about family and the conversation turns to Dolly. Gladys asks him about his intentions toward Dolly and he intimates he really likes her but doesn't know what she wants. Gladys invites him to meet Papa Dear at a meeting and tells him Dolly will be there. Gladys tells him she likes him and gives him a hug.

Questions

- What makes Gladys so interested in the Inspector's report?
- Why does Errol's face cloud over at the mention of his family?
- Gladys manipulates Errol to some extent. How does he feel about Dolly?
- Predict what you think might happen in Melbourne.

Act Two

Scene Seven: The Petition

The three women are in a *'draughty hall'* and we learn from their conversation that Dolly has a nursing scholarship in Melbourne. Nan is to look after Regina. Errol comes in and Gladys says she invited him. Gladys drags Nan away so Dolly and Errol can talk. Errol tells her and realises he has been a fool and apologises. He also tells her that he loves her but she rejects him. He respects her decision and asks if they can be friends.

Nan and Gladys come back and Dolly tells Nan she has followed her advice and rejected Errol. Nan has a turn and Errol offers to drive her home to Mooroopna. Dolly sees Nan talking directly to Errol for the first time. Nan learns Errol is a fake Fisher and he was originally a Germanic Vischer but the family changed their name during the war. Nan and Dolly realise what this means and Nan kisses him on the cheek.

They learn Papa Dear is not coming and Gladys gets up and makes a speech. She reads it with increasing confidence. She even adds to the petition and whips the crowd up. Nan notices Errol and Dolly looking at each other longingly. The family hug Gladys and in a dream sequence Nan sees Errol and Dolly married. Back in reality Nan tells Dolly to marry him and it ends with blessings all round. Papa Dear arrives and the play ends with the song *Que Sera, Sera*.

Questions

- This scene is very positive. List all the positive things that happen to the characters.
- Summarise what Gladys says in her petition speech.
- How have each of the characters learnt that even diverse experiences and attitudes can unite through opening individuals up to new and positive experiences? How do emotion and logic interplay through the decisions individual characters make?
- Research the song *Que Sera, Sera* (Whatever will be, will be) on a site such as LyricZZ.com. What relevance does the Jay Livingstone/ Ray Evans song hold for the play as a whole? This chart topping song was popularised by Doris Day and appeared in Hitchcock's film *The Man Who Knew Too Much* in 1956.

SETTING

Most of the action in the drama occurs around the humpy. They share this community with people of similar experiences and it is Errol, the Caucasian who is the outsider here. It is important, for example, to Dolly who tells Errol when he invites her to Melbourne,

> 'And as far as what you're offering...no thank you. This is my place. I'm staying, right here with my mum, and my nan. (p172)

or as Gladys clearly points out to the Chairman at the council meeting,

> 'I'm not an interloper – I belong here – this is my land! (p180)

This is despite the hardships such as flood and mice at the humpy. Here they have a certain freedom but Harrison doesn't gloss over the problems at the Flats, including the goomees and domestic violence. When they move to the pre-fabricated housing at Rumbalara, Nan doesn't like it very much and gets a cough. They also seem to lose a bit of their identity and contact with nature.

One place at the Flats is repeatedly mentioned as ominous – the cork trees. Dolly is repeatedly warned to stay away from the place and it is where the drunks hang out. For example her Nan says,

> 'If I catch you going past those cork trees – '

These are also where her cousin, Leroy, hangs out and he causes much angst when he drunkenly rapes Dolly. This dramatic and traumatic experience happens here and this negative experience doesn't stop her from her ultimate goal(s).

Other scenes are played in various places such as the hall in Shepparton, the hall in Melbourne and the park bench. These are more for plot enhancement rather than anything to do with the structural integrity of the play. One other setting that should be mentioned is the constant use of the dream sequence where characters seem to segue into various possibilities then return to reality. This is done visually with the use of the theatre lighting and in one case a screen. Perhaps we can consider the dreams as experiences as well.

Questions

- How does the setting at the Flats contribute to the 'feel' of the play?
- Why does Harrison set most of the scenes around the humpy? Think about shared emotional experiences.
- How are the cork trees made ominous in the script?
- Discuss how Melbourne is portrayed and why the different environment might alter experiences.

CHARACTER ANALYSIS

- Nan Dear
- Gladys Banks
- Dolly Banks
- Errol Fisher
- Other characters

Nan Dear

Nan Dear is the most pragmatic of the three women and she is the character who most often moderates the dreams and ideals of Gladys and Dolly. This is not to say that Nan doesn't want the best for her girls. For example, she dreams of Dolly marrying Errol after she is satisfied his intentions are honourable. Nan is also protective of Dolly and warns her repeatedly about hanging around the cork trees. She is also very proud of Gladys when she goes to the council meeting and when she presents the petition at the end of the play.

Nan's cynical approach to the everyday problems of Aborigines in general and Aboriginal women in particular is born from years of witnessing racism first hand. She has also suffered at the hands of white authorities having had Gladys removed to a white family as a servant. Nan has also suffered personally as we see when she shares her secret with Dolly after the rape,

> 'No, Dolly – See, I was walking home, taking a short cut, and – and – and the lad – he took advantage of me... (p187)

Nan Dear is not all cynicism and pragmatism as she has a good sense of humour as well. We see this with her pointed comments about how Aboriginal people are treated, like being served last at the butchers. Nan Dear also has a temper and we see it occasionally such as her 'outburst',

'And what bloody good would that do?! Daydreams! (p154)

or when she throws eggs and yells at the officious rent man, Mr Coody,

'I don't care what you think! You and your visiting hours. Your rules. No singalongs after dark. Your spying. You mister, can go to blazes! I'll give you 'one'...' (p186)

Nan is also reasonable though as we see with her later treatment of Errol. We understand her earlier behaviour after her reasons are explained. She is understanding of Errol and Dolly's relationship at the end and is able to admit she misunderstood when her reasoning is exposed as flawed. Nan is also very understanding of Aboriginal people. For example, look at what she says about the goomees,

'What you call them? Shame! They might be drinkers, but they're still our people.'

and

'Show some respect, girl. They've had it hard those lads.' (p139)

This understanding comes from a lifetime of experiences and her overall view of things. Her comments are sometimes tinged with bitterness as she recounts the hardships of her youth. Look at the scene where she is talking to Dolly about her home in the Murray River,

> 'They forced us to leave. Forced us to leave Cummeragunja. Our home.' (p126)

and she doesn't continue to answer questions about 'that business'.

Nan knows about the world and how it works for Aboriginals but is nonetheless pleased at the conclusion of events in the play. She shows a great inner strength to survive and witness the start of a changing reality for her family.

Questions

- How do we know Nan Dear cares for Gladys and Dolly?
- Give one example of her cynicism and state how this may be born out of experience.
- How do we see the Aboriginal experience in her sense of belonging to the land?
- List three events in her life that expose the struggles of an Aboriginal woman in the middle of the twentieth century.
- Why does Nan Dear criticise Gladys' 'ideas' and 'daydreams'?
- Give ONE example of Nan's temper.
- In one paragraph show how Nan feels about her Aboriginality and the Aboriginality of the people she loves. State how this is translated into her day to day way of dealing with the world, especially other people.

Gladys Banks

Gladys is the most positive and optimistic of the three women in *Rainbow's End* and is the most hopeful for the future. We first think she is a bit odd with her obsession with seeing the Queen on her visit to Australia. When she is criticised by Nan Dear for this, we see her inner strength and passion,

> 'I'm not hurting anyone, am I? It's a moment I'll remember... to see our pretty young monarch and the Duke. I'm not going to miss it for all the tea in China! (p124)

Even when Gladys doesn't get close to the Queen we see that she is undaunted by the experience. We also see her intelligence when she is able to answer the quiz questions. The fact she cannot read or write is highlighted twice but this is not due to her intelligence or ability but opportunity. As she tells Errol,

> 'but then the mission managers were terrible and it was all downhill, and I got sent off to work for a family. A family of six and a big house to look after – who had time for learning? Then Len and I married...' (p184)

Gladys always maintains her hopes and ambitions for Dolly and she says clearly that she wants for her daughter what every mother wants for her daughter. She instils a pride in Dolly although Dolly does question why they live in a humpy if they are just like everyone else.

Gladys is the driving force behind much of the action in the realm of positive change in the play. She responds to setbacks and always keeps in mind what she sees as important. One example of this is when she loses the encyclopaedias that she loved so much and worked so hard for. When they are destroyed in the flood she says,

> 'No! No! They're only possessions. And what do they matter? People is what matters.' (p176)

Gladys knows that she has to be resilient to withstand the knocks that she has had. She often surprises others with her strength. One example of this is when she goes to the council meeting to speak her mind on Aboriginal housing and is ejected. Nan says,

> 'I didn't really think you had it in you, daught' (p182)

She also makes them all proud at the Melbourne meeting when Nan Dear tells her,

> 'You done us proud, Gladys. Your dad'd be... real proud of ya.' (p198)

Gladys is also resilient enough to admit her mistakes as she does with Errol when she apologises,

> 'I'm sorry about last time, Errol, I wasn't so smart then. I treated you unfairly.' (p183)

but she turns this into a positive by inviting Errol back into their world and it enables him to eventually reunite with Dolly, showing she is able to learn from her experiences.

The overriding impression we get of Gladys is her love of family and her hopes for Dolly. This is exposed in her dream sequences such as the one where she sees Dolly graduate,

'The lights change for a dream sequence. GLADYS sees DOLLY in a robe and clapboard hat...The lighting fades back to reality. GLADYS looks around fearful that her 'daydream' has been witnessed, but it hasn't' (p134)

Gladys is a strong Aboriginal female in a period when this wasn't necessarily an advantage.

Questions

- Give two specific examples of Gladys' resilience.
- How do we see her hopes for herself and her daughter? Give one language example in your response.
- Choose one interaction between Gladys and a whitefella (eg Errol, the bank manager). Analyse what this shows about her and its impact on the play. You could also state what it shows about Australia during the 1950s and attitudes toward Aboriginals.
- Give an example of Gladys' resolve to conclude issues.
- Discuss Gladys' ambitions for Dolly. Are they realistic for that period in Australian history?
- How, through dialogue, do we see her love for her mum and Dolly?
- Analyse one dream sequence and consider what it adds to our knowledge of Gladys and how this dream might form part of the human experience.

Dolly Banks

Dolly is the young daughter of Gladys and we follow her path to becoming a woman and mother in the play. Even the two older women in the play get used to the idea of her being a woman,

'She's not a girl' (p176)

This seventeen/eighteen year old who excels at school is also beautiful and this is commented on throughout the play. She is full of hope about life and excited about her romance with Errol. She seems to have some of the usual teenage problems with authority but she is generally respectful and polite.

Dolly has an endearing nature but is also realistic about the world while still having hopes. Her mother helps here by encouraging her dreams. One example of this is when she says in response to her mother telling her to do her maths homework,

'Yeah, so I can be a bookkeeper... in the laundry.' (153)

She also questions her place in the world. Look at the dialogue with her mother in Act One Scene Nine,

'Nan thinks soap and water, and you think that books and school, are the answer to everything...It's me that gets stones thrown at her when I walk down the street. It's me that gets snide remarks.' (p162)

But Gladys tells her not to be 'shamed'. Dolly suffers two major shaming events on the night of the ball. The first is when Nancy (in a voice-over) tells how Dolly's dress is made from curtain material her mother had thrown away at the tip. The second, of course, is the rape at the cork trees. She seems to bounce back from these events. The first one is changed by Errol at the river when he tells her he loves her and wants to marry her. At first she is cheered but leaves him because of lack of respect. The second incident Dolly seems to overcome through time passing and the birth of her child, Regina. She is able to finally talk about it with Nan Dear,

'Nan. About that night, at the cork trees –'. (p187)

and she appears to have a bright future from this point with her new nursing career and the scholarship to complete it. She also has Errol at the end and everyone's blessing to that union.

Dolly is a very positive character in the play and all the hopes and ambitions of Gladys have been embedded in her. Like her mother, she is very resilient and can overcome adversity. We get a sense that her tale of love and hope is a tale that could be repeated. She takes her mother's hopes and carries them to fruition. We see her mother in her in one of her final lines,

'It'll be all right.' (p199)

which she has adopted from Gladys.

Dolly is the more modern, educated Aboriginal woman who provides a positive role model to the audience. She is the epitome of dreams becoming reality.

Questions

- How does the audience see Dolly at the beginning of the play? Does this change by the conclusion of *Rainbow's End*?
- Discuss one experience that changes Dolly's view of an individual significantly.
- Why does Dolly initially reject Errol? Is she right to do this?
- Why does she again reject Errol's offer at the river? What does this say about her as a person?
- List three positive experiences that involve her and how they impact on her attitudes and beliefs?

Errol Fisher

Errol Fisher is a whitefella in his twenties who comes along, by mistake, to the humpy one day. He is a visiting encyclopaedia salesman and Gladys says when they first meet him,

> 'He seems nice. Real polite' (p136)

and this is a good indicator of Errol's character. He is a nice young man who only has good intentions but is naïve and doesn't understand many of the situations he gets himself into. While the three women see Errol as the city boy from Melbourne he is far from sophisticated and though Nan says cities are 'full of sin', Errol isn't.

Errol is always nice to Dolly and we know he is attracted to her in a positive way. He says such things as,

> 'What do you want to do? A girl like you...you could do anything you want.' (p141)

and at the ball,

'That's cause you're the prettiest girl here.' (p165)

While he seems oblivious to the black/white divide Dolly tries to point it out to him but he perseveres anyway. His problem initially is the lack of understanding of her situation when he asks her to go to Melbourne with him,

> 'Yes. To the city. We can get married. You could get a job. We can get a little flat. Wouldn't you like that? A sweet little flat with a balcony and a sitting room and a kitchen with a real stove and a new-fangled Kelvinator and water on tap...That'd have to be better than the river...' (p171)

He doesn't understand her links to the land and her family. He is an outsider and white and they mistrust him on a basic level. For example Gladys and Nan drive him off after the rape assuming it was him, showing how past experience influences the present.

This does not deter him however and he persists with his good-nature and love for Dolly undiminished. He even says to Gladys when she tells him Dolly's changed,

> 'Then I'll have to change too. I'll prove to her I can. That I'm worthy of her'. (p184)

Errol doesn't understand her idea of family as his is quite different. His father wants Errol to call him 'sir' and his mother,

> 'well, she has these funny ideas sometimes...rather, my dad thinks they're funny ideas. Take this – she wants to get a job. She says she's at home, with nothing to do but bake and dust –' (p170)

This is very different from life on the Flats. Errol however persists and when Dolly rejects him at the hall in Melbourne he still retains his dignity, even after telling her he was wrong about her family,

> 'Then I'll respect your decision...And I wish you all the happiness in the world. You, and your lovely little daughter. And I hope we can at least be friends.' (p193)

It is this basic decency that gets him Dolly in the end. By offering to help Nan she comes to know and like him,

> 'I can recognise a good man when I see one' (p198)

and Errol is very happy as he and Dolly 'hold each others hands and look at each other adoringly.' This is a fitting end for two decent people who are in love. Errol has earnt his position in the family and they have accepted him.

Questions

- How do we know from the beginning of the play that Errol is basically a decent person?
- Discuss three incidents where he shows his naivety about life. State what each shows about his character.
- Do you think his invitation to Dolly to marry him and move to Melbourne is disrespectful or just a misunderstanding or both?
- Explain your response fully and include quotes and/or specific examples.
- Do you think Dolly is too harsh when she tells him about their relationship,

    'No...it's...impossible.' ?

- How is Errol's family different to Dolly's? Think about the different experiences when growing up, the way they see the world and how their beliefs are very different. Do you think they may have any similarities?
- What qualities enable Errol to eventually earn the right to belong to the Dear/Banks family?

OTHER CHARACTERS

The other characters in *Rainbow's End* highlight different issues. For example the **bank manager** shows the patronising attitude that was common in the country at that time but still helps her with the application form. His prejudice is so ingrained that he doesn't even think about offering her a cup of tea when he pours one for himself.

The **inspector** shows the good intentions but basic uselessness of government in seeing and knowing the problem but being unable to act in a useful manner. He has lots of words but little else, especially with his talk of assimilation. He is also a figure that causes great distress and anxiety in the community because he has the power to remove children, as he does with Ester's.

Mr Coody, the **rent collector**, shows little respect for the women and he looks at the pregnant Dolly 'with disdain'. He is an officious man with little understanding and regard for those in his care. He is pompous and says things like,

> 'It is very much my concern. Everything to do with the habitation of this establishment is my concern.' (p185)

The **policeman** is a very minor role to show how the Aborigines view officialdom. He is also ineffective in what he does. The final figure is **Papa Dear** who makes an appearance in a dream sequence but is otherwise off doing good work in the Aboriginal cause. He is basically absent from the women's lives.

THEMATIC CONCERNS

■ Texts and Human Experience
■ The Human Experience of Belonging
■ Aboriginal Themes

Texts and Human Experience

Rainbow's End is a close examination of the effect of the human experience on a small group of individuals who portray a wider issue in Australian society throughout this period of history. We can examine the various experiences of the characters in the play and come to some conclusions about Harrison's purpose in writing the drama. We should also bear in mind the experiences that Harrison brings to her work, which would influence not only the content but also our perspective when viewing the play.

The physical experiences are the obvious contrast in the 1950s between the Aboriginals and the 'whitefellas'. Skin colour meant something in that period and we can see the obvious racism in the play based on colour. The experiences in the Aboriginal community, which seems defined by their skin colour, obviously impact on their view of the world and how they deal with it. They are treated as second class citizens and have few rights. The paternal attitude of the representatives of authority are feared and treated with suspicion because of past experiences (the mission) and current ones such as the removal of children.

We can also appreciate the experience of the Aboriginal people being removed from their land and the cost of this. Nan misses her traditional lands and often thinks about returning. In the lands around the river they are isolated and displaced which leads to many negative social experiences such as the drinking and violence. Rumbalara is seen by the authorities as the solution but the attempt to assimilate the Aboriginals is more like cultural destruction and an attempt to eliminate Aboriginal identity.

Dolly's experiences with society are invariably negative because of her race. Psychologically and emotionally she is scarred from the racism she encounters and the way she is seen in a society that values only one cultural experience. No matter how much she involves herself in the cultural norms and experiences of the times, e.g. education, dress, Dolly and her kin can't ever be fully of that culture because of the colour of their skin. The experiences they suffer because of this don't necessarily deter them fully because of the strength of their character and indeed the negative experiences make them stronger, but they have to be better and work harder. We see that Gladys, for example, can never reach her full potential because of her experiences at the mission, the denial of her education and the genuine reduction in opportunity.

Emotionally these experiences leave scars that need to be overcome and Harrison allows us to enter this world as well through the experiential insights shown through the drama and dialogue. One example would be the rape scene and its aftermath, when Errol gets the blame and we see the angst in Nan and Gladys when Dolly refutes their claim. That whole night is an emotional rollercoaster for Dolly and Errol and we think it could be the end of that relationship, despite indications they feel deeply for each other. We know from our studies that emotions are primary drivers of motivation and human behaviours and Harrison uses this to show us dramatically how individuals and in this case a family are impacted.

We cannot discount the experiences shared by the family, as these unite them and we see the strong bonds between them and the support this offers. This extends culturally to the Aboriginal community and one example of this is the 'goomees' who have the understanding of the elders because of what they have had to endure despite their drinking and negative influence in the community. The cultural experiences which are also spiritual are reinforced by the communities' experiences as they have to endure colonisation and government policies that have attempted to enforce 'assimilation'.

So, how does the experience of Errol fit into this pattern? He is undoubtedly naïve about the ways of the world and the Aboriginal community but what differentiates Errol from the other 'whitefellas' is his ability to adapt and be open to new ideas and ways of thinking. He knows his father has stereotypical thinking of the 1950s but Errol doesn't blindly follow. He learns to see Dolly as a person whom he loves rather than someone who needs to be rescued. Dolly is portrayed as an independent woman with skills of her own, a mother, a student and a person who is trying to determine her own future and choose her experiences rather than have them thrust upon her.

These experiences have been recorded by Harrison based on real experiences from history and recalled events in Aboriginal history. It is interesting that she then fictionalises these events – a form of narrative storytelling – and brings them to life for modern audiences to experience. As we read in the context she writes a story focused on one family to make the experience personal but we can extrapolate these ideas into a wider cultural perspective. This is her purpose: to explore the effect of paternalistic practices on the Aboriginal people(s).

Rainbow's End needs to be read and understood as a dramatic piece and to appreciate the full experience we need to recognise the theatricality of the piece. Harrison uses drama to convey the emotional experience of the characters as well as the narrative line so that the audience can empathise with the characters and come to some understanding of their story. We see Nan's anger, Dolly's pain and feel when Gladys is rejected and rebuffed. This is our experience in the theatre, so pay heed to the stage directions and the dream sequences etc. that form the theatrical part of the script.

Questions

- How does a sense of Aboriginal experience unite the three women in the play?
- Harrison shows how Aboriginal people belong to the land. How does she do this and how is it part of their experience?
- Discuss ONE negative experience in the play and the effect it has on a belief or attitude.
- Discuss ONE positive experience in the play and the effect it has on a belief or attitude.
- How does the concept of storytelling influence the content of the play? Give specific example/s from *Rainbow's End*.
- How might the experience of seeing the play change your experience of reading it?

The Human Experience of Belonging

Belonging is an idea that permeates *Rainbow's End* in a variety of ways. One is obviously the Aboriginal heritage and values that we read of in the play. Another is the importance of belonging to a particular group within that culture, such as the people down on the Flats. Another is family and the associations that go with that concept. We can also relate the idea of wanting to belong to a society as a whole and the advantages that go with belonging to that group and, conversely, being excluded from that group. In this drama we also have an interesting reversal of that idea when 'whitefella' Errol is excluded from the Aboriginal family when he wants to marry Dolly.

The sense of belonging in the Aboriginal community is strong. They identify with their culture and are proud of it, wanting a realisation of the problems they face. In the play we see how they belong to this cultural tradition and it strengthens them and binds them together. We see this when Nan takes a rabbit over to Ester because she is pregnant and is also suffering from abuse at the hands of her 'whitefella husband'. This sense of unity is not just felt by the people who live at the Flats but extends to the wider Aboriginal community, even those Dolly calls,

> 'those townie types of cross-over Aboriginals' (p149)

This Aboriginal heritage means they all belong to one cohort, as Nan reminds Dolly,

> 'What you call them? Shame! They might be drinkers but they're still our people' (p139)

This sense of belonging to a community heritage also extends to the land for Aborigines. Look at how bitter and displaced Nan feels about being taken away from Cummeragunja and the loss of her freedom to 'do things our way'. This tie to the land is as strong as the tie to family. Nan talks about going home to die and having a 'feed of' swan eggs. This is a shared experience with her community and she longs for her land and her people.

The sense of belonging to a family is also very strong in *Rainbow's End*. Dolly rejects Errol for that very reason when he offers to take her to Melbourne and marry her. She says clearly to him,

> 'But...a real home? A real home is where there are people looking after each other' (p172)

and

> 'This is my place. I'm staying right here with my mum and my nan. (p172)

Errol doesn't understand how important family is to Dolly, partly because it is beyond his experience, until the end of the play when he says,

> 'I realise I was wrong. For example, I will come up here, if you want. Because where you belong, and your family, is important. To you and to me' (p193)

This realisation underlines the importance of family to Dolly and the Dear/Banks family in general. We also hear Dolly talk about all her 'brothers'. We see all through the play the family's love for each other despite minor disagreements. They are always there for each other. This sense of identity as a family and community gives them strength.

This strength is needed as they have to overcome much in the course of their lives. They live in a society that doesn't value them or their culture and they suffer for not belonging to mainstream of white Australia. They contend with racism and ignorance while still trying to make a life for themselves in that society. They have little other choice unless they opt out completely like the goomees or sacrifice their identity. Even Gladys and Dolly argue over the racism they suffer,

> 'Have you, Mum? Have you learnt not to be shamed by them? I thought not. You're always telling me to stick up for myself, but when do you, eh?' (p162)

We see their exclusion in various ways, housing, jobs, education, and we also learn how families were separated. This sense of not belonging is alienating and difficult to overcome. We see some great resilience from these women to continue to hope and dream as they do. Even when they get new housing at Rumbalara it is inappropriate and over-supervised. The inspector talks of assimilation and 'being absorbed into the community'. This means, according to the inspector, learning to live like us'. This is cultural genocide, not true belonging.

Rainbow's End also examines a different aspect of belonging when Errol is excluded from the family because he is white and untrusted. Nan never likes him until the end of the last scene and he is blamed for the rape because he is white and cultural/personal history suggests it was him. He feels badly over his exclusion and is ecstatic at the end because he is accepted and gets their blessing. Errol even accepts Regina unquestioningly even though she obviously is not his child. This acceptance is developed through his experiences.

Aboriginal Themes

While the main concept set for study is Human Experiences it is useful to look at some of the details of Aboriginal issues that can be linked to this main theme. For the Aborigines in the play it is a struggle to belong, especially on their own terms in a white world that wants to take away their Aboriginality. In *Rainbow's End* we learn that people have been displaced from their traditional lands, families have been torn apart and traditional ways of life are discouraged. These people's experiences are very different from the traditional ways but they try and cling to some of the culture that sustains them.

One clear example of the white view of Aboriginal life is the inspector, a 'well-dressed white man' who inspects their dwelling and asks questions about their lifestyle while constantly taking notes. He talks to them of assimilation,

> 'The Aborigine needs to be absorbed into the community. But how can he be absorbed until he learns to live like us? I will recommend assimilation, in my report. It is a vexed issue to be sure, but someone must take leadership.' (p152)

The Inspector thinks that because of the beliefs he has from his own experience, they will be better trying to be the same as him, but the text illustrates belonging can also be about diversity within a group, especially a large one like a society, which needs variety to grow. Harrison shows it can be difficult to reconcile contrasting beliefs and attitudes about the world, yet she does manage some 'reconciliation' with the positive conclusion between Errol and Dolly.

We have already examined the idea of belonging to a culture, but you may also wish to think about what this entails, the experiences this generates and the responsibilities it brings. Look at Nan for example. She is the matriarch of the group, a respected elder, who has no male support and tries to keep the family and the community together.

As well as highlighting the overt problems of housing, education and displacement, *Rainbow's End* shows dramatically the insidious nature of racism. This may not be overt but can appear in subtle forms that alienate individuals. Harrison shows us that experiences with racism can be an undercurrent that separates people. It is not all negative though as Harrison does show us that love, i.e. positive experiences, can break down these barriers.

Overall, the play highlights issues that still relate to modern indigenous lives that give it an immediacy and relevance on stage. Some of the concerns are still with communities from the 1950s and this must provide thought for analysis. Harrison uses Aboriginality in the play to show how belonging to a group can be a very positive experience but how isolation and rejection can destroy lives, create conflict and endanger cultures that don't fit the accepted norms of that period.

Questions

- How is a sense of Aboriginal heritage conveyed in the play?
- Harrison shows Aboriginal people have a different set of beliefs to the 'whitefellas'. How does she do this?
- What benefits are shown from belonging to a family?
- What problems are illustrated when groups/ individuals are excluded from another group/ society. Give specific examples of experiences from the text and one other source.
- How does the concept of racism prevent belonging? Give specific example/s from Rainbow's End.
- Imagine you are Errol. How do you feel after Dolly rejects you and your offer of marriage and a better life? Discuss whether you think she was fair in her response to you and state why you don't give up hope because of this negative experience.
- What qualities create a sense of belonging for individuals in the play?

LANGUAGE ANALYSIS

Harrison's *Rainbow's End* uses generally colloquial language and some 1950s slang terms such as bodgies and widgies. She also uses some Aboriginal terms such as *mamel* (carpet snake), *gubba* (whitefella), *goomees* (drinkers) etc. this use of generally colloquial language makes the play accessible to a wide range of audiences. The subject matter is also topical and touches on things familiar to most Australians and a wide range of indigenous peoples.

Some small fragments of more formal language can be found in the Inspector's report and the petition. One example is,

> 'Her Majesty, Queen Elizabeth the Second, Queen of England and her Territories. We humbly present this petition to you'. (p196)

This language is not ubiquitous and is only used as an exemplar to show the differences in official language and the language of the people.

Much of the dialogue revolves and evolves around the three women and their interaction. Here we see how close they are by the way that they can finish each other's sentences and know how the others will respond. We see how much they care for each other and many scenes are very emotive, none more so than the scene after Dolly has been raped and returns to the humpy. Here we see Gladys 'panicking' and she asks,

> 'Dolly, what is it? Dolly please? (p175)

In this scene it is the wailing that creates the aural drama for the audience but it is full of dramatist's instruction. Here the actions especially add to the dramatic impact as the scene is so emotive Dolly can't speak. In this scene we also get another technique that Harrison commonly uses – song. Here, it is the theme song 'Que Sera, Sera'. Harrison uses song frequently in the play and we get tunes such as 'Somewhere Over the Rainbow', big band swing music, 'A Girl Like You' by Cliff Richard and the Shadows etc. These add emotion and context to the scenes and reinforce the words and action.

Another technique that Harrison incorporates into Rainbow's End is the use of the radio as a means of communicating with the actors and the audience. Through radio, which is placed at the beginning of many scenes to set tone, we learn such things as how intelligent Gladys is (through Pick-a-Box questions). We also learn about her 'radio moment' when she is ejected from the council meeting and the Queen's visit. It gives us different perspectives such as the reporter's view of the new Aboriginal Housing. The radio is also a source of amusement and frustration with its fading valve.

Dream sequences are also a major focus in this contemporary indigenous play. They show characters' hopes and dreams for the future and are integrated and relevant to the action. These dream sequences are quite numerous in the play as the characters have many hopes and dreams for themselves and their family members. Gladys has many 'ideas' which are criticised by Nan. Gladys especially has aspirations for Dolly as we see in her dream sequence when,

> 'The lights change for a dream sequence. GLADYS sees DOLLY in a robe and clapboard hat...The lighting fades

back to reality. GLADYS looks around fearful that her 'daydream' has been witnessed, but it hasn't'. (p134)

These dream sequences' frequent occurrence allow the audience to see some of the 'secrets' these women have. For example, we see Dolly dream of winning the Miss Mooroopna-Shepparton Ball,

> 'A sash is hung over DOLLY'S shoulder. DOLLY is astounded – so excited.' (p166)

and Nan's dream sequence where she sees,

> 'Wedding bells and confetti as DOLLY and ERROL – pram in the middle – get hitched.' (p198)

Other interesting features of the play are the use of voice-over and the numerous roles the actor playing Errol has to undertake. The voice-over gives flexibility to the stagecraft and allows disparate elements to enter the play. This technique allows the plot to evolve chronologically while allowing the pace to be maintained without unnecessary explanatory scenes, for example Nancy's voice-over at the Ball,

> 'Why, if it isn't Miss Dolores Banks herself. Love your dress, Dolly. Love the fabric. [With a giggle] My mother quite liked it too. When it was our sunroom curtains. But, you know, I thought we took them to the tip.' (p166)

This voice-over is the catalyst for much of the conflict that follows. This use of stagecraft also extends to the use of the actor playing Errol as other characters. Other than the four main parts, all the others parts are small and are placed so that 'Errol' can perform them. These are parts such as the bank manager, the rent man, the inspector and the policeman. They are all male roles that are easily filled. The offstage voices are more disparate and could be pre-recorded.

It is also interesting to recognise how Harrison concludes the play on a positive note with all the main characters fulfilling some part of their hopes and aspirations. Dolly, for example, has a nursing scholarship and is to marry Errol. Gladys has learnt how to read and has seen the best for her daughter. This is very positive and offers the audience more than problems and negativity. *Rainbow's End* offers Aboriginal solutions to Aboriginal problems through the actions of individuals.

Questions

- Discuss how the use of the songs contribute to the overall impact of the play. How do songs affect an audience? Think about how they marry to scenes and characters.
- Why would Harrison use mainly colloquial language in the play?
- Harrison uses some Aboriginal terms. Why would she keep these to a minimum?
- Discuss how the medium of the radio is used in the play. How is it integral to the plot and character development?
- Choose one dream sequence and analyse it carefully. Describe its impact on the play as a whole and how effective it would be on stage for an audience.
- Discuss one other piece of Harrison's stagecraft and analyse its effectiveness.
- How effective is the conclusion to *Rainbow's End*? Is it realistic?

THE ESSAY

The essay consists of the basic form of an introduction, body paragraphs and conclusion. The esssay has been the subject of numerous texts and you should have the basic form well in hand. As teachers, the point we would emphasise would be to link the paragraphs both to each other and back to your argument (which should directly respond to the question). Of course, ensure your argument is logical and sustained.

Make sure you use specific examples and that your quotes are accurate. To ensure that you respond to the question, make sure you plan carefully and are sure what relevant point each paragraph is making. It is solid technique to actually 'tie up' each point by explicitly coming back to the question.

When composing an essay the basic conventions of the form are:

- State your argument, outline the points to be addressed and perhaps have a brief definition.

A solid structure for each paragraph is:
- Topic sentence (*the main idea and its link to the previous paragraph/ argument*)
- Explanation/ discussion of the point including links between texts if applicable.
- Detailed evidence (*Close textual reference – quotes, incidents and technique discussion.*)
- Tie up by restating the point's relevance to argument/ question

- Summary of points
- Final sentence that restates your argument

As well as this basic structure, you will need to focus on:

Audience – for the essay the audience must be considered formal unless specifically stated otherwise. Therefore, your language must reflect the audience. This gives you the opportunity to use the jargon and vocabulary that you have learnt in English. For the audience ensure your introduction is clear and has impact. Avoid slang or colloquial language including contractions (like 'doesn't', 'e.g.', 'etc.').

Purpose – the purpose of the essay is to answer the question given. The examiner evaluates how well you can make an argument and understand the module's issues and its text(s). An essay is solidly structured so its composer can analyse ideas. This is where you earn marks. It does not retell the story or state the obvious.

Communication – Take a few minutes to plan the essay. If you rush into your answer it is almost certain you will not make the most of the brief 40 minutes to show all you know about the question. More likely you will include irrelevant details that do not gain you marks but waste your precious time. Remember an essay is formal so **do not** do the following: story-tell, list and number points, misquote, use slang or colloquial language, be vague, use non-sentences or fail to address the question.

PLAN:

Don't even think about starting without one!

Introduce...

the texts you are using in the response

Argument: The human experience is affected by:
- Idea One
- Idea Two
- Idea Three

You need to let the marker know what texts you are discussing. You can start with a definition but it can come in the first paragraph of the body. You MUST state your argument in response to the question and the points you will cover as part of it. Wait until the end of the response to give it!

Idea One – Aspect of human experience as outlined in the textual material, e.g. physical impact.

Idea Two – Another aspect of human experience as outlined in the textual material, e.g. psychological impact.

- explain the idea
- where and how is it shown in the prescribed text?
- where and how is it shown in related text 1?

Idea Three – People's sense of experience is affected by context and environment

- explain the idea
- where and how shown in the prescribed text?
- where and how shown in related text 1?

You can use the things you have learned to organise the essay. For each one, you say where you saw this in your prescribed text and where in related text(s).

Two or three ideas are usually enough as you can explore them in detail.

- Summary of two key ideas
- Final sentence that restates your argument

Make sure your conclusion restates your argument. It does not have to be too long.

MODEL ESSAY OUTLINE

> **To what extent are human experiences significant in the set text?**
>
> **From your studies respond to this question using your set text and at ONE piece of other textual material**

This essay needs to be attacked in a manner that responds to the question and shows ALL your knowledge about the text. The question lends itself to a close study of Jane Harrison's *Rainbow's End* as the text does show how the human experience is integral to life and how it shapes our other experiences and interaction with the world.

An introduction might be written:

> Human experiences are important in Harrison's play *Rainbow's End* and the two related texts Lawrence's film *Jindabyne* and Ed Sheeran's song *Castle on the Hill*. These texts show how human experiences are integral to human existence and bring more meaning to one's life. Life is about experiences that challenge us and define how we see the world. They shape our beliefs and attitudes and can be confronting at the same time. Without experiences our lives would be empty and meaningless.

Your essay should then follow the outlined plan and develop these ideas. This gives you the opportunity to link the texts and fully develop each of the ideas.

ANNOTATED RELATED MATERIAL: DIFFERENT STUDIES OF HUMAN EXPERIENCES

Jindabyne – Ray Lawrence

Jindabyne is an Australian film that captures a wide array of human experiences. It touches on the ideas mentioned in the introduction to this text in a number of detailed instances. We can begin by considering the following before beginning a detailed examination of the narrative.

The collective human experience:

- Aboriginality and the spiritual;
- The Fishermen and their code;
- The reaction of the townsfolk;
- Media response;
- Interaction with the natural world.

Individual Experience:

- An individual character's response to the body – choose one;
- The killer;
- Response to the revelations;
- Past experiences and how they impact on current experiences;
- Reaction to loss – emotional;
- Assumptions about life.

We can now look at the plot to help us understand each of these issues. *Jindabyne* begins with the sound of a radio being tuned and the Australian feel of the movie is immediate with the theme music for the ABC news. Lawrence emphasises the isolation by having the radio not tune in correctly for an unknown female character, forcing her to use the cassette player. With this unusual beginning we know that her experience is not going to be positive.

We then pan to the rocks slowly where Gregory, our killer, sits patiently in a truck with the engine running watching the road. We know he is prepared for this as he has binoculars. He sees an Aboriginal girl, Susan O'Connor, driving and she is the one fiddling with the radio. He chases her down and forces her to stop. He moves toward her as we see a long shot of how isolated they are. We see his face in her window looming above her and screaming about the electricity coming down from the mountains. This film is no murder mystery, as we know from the beginning that the murderer is Gregory the electrician. This is about the experiences of the other characters in the film and how they respond to current experiences.

The Kane family, Stewart, Claire and son Tom, is waking. Claire pretends to sleep, before waking suddenly and being affectionate with Tom. Stewart and Tom head out fishing. The scene doesn't feel quite right and there is some emotional tension between Stewart and Claire that is unspoken due to what they have experienced in the past. Claire had a complicated past when she was pregnant with Tom. When she finds she is pregnant again, she becomes emotional and slightly unstable.

As the film builds we see the complex pasts of the characters and their interactions in the confinement of the small town. The fishing trip is a break from this and extremely important in their lives.

We see some of the emotional instability in characters such as Caylin-Calandria, who with Tom, has some issues at school. Along with Caylin-Calandria, Claire and Jude also have issues but in a nicely framed shot of the three female characters, we see them conform as members of a close knit group. The sacrifice they make is similar to Gregory's but on a different scale. Note the connection here and how each one is to get back to order and societal norms. This is the collective experience for all the characters.

At the Kanes' home the tensions are obvious from their past experiences but they contain it for appearances' sake. Occasionally, the tension reaches breaking point and the experience strains the superficial approach. The tension builds at home and the fishing trip seems like a good opportunity to break the cycle.

When we see Gregory dump Susan O'Connor's body in the river, we know that the fishing and her death will interact.

The next morning, the fishermen head off for their one big trip of the year and the sign 'Gone fishing' is put in the garage window. We see Billy on the phone to Elissa and putting the sign the wrong way round in the window shows his immaturity. They have already said they are taking him away to make a man of him. The four men have a few beers on the way and talk as they travel through the landscape. They intend to give Billy the experience they think he needs as a 'man' — a cultural rite of passage.

The men arrive and the high-tension electricity wires punctuate the wilderness. They begin to hike toward the valley. It's a long walk in and the terrain is hilly and difficult. They stop on the way and again we see Billy's naivety when Stewart says 'Listen to that' meaning the silence but he can't, as he has his earphones in. It is part of the break in tension of the film that they commune with nature. This experiential break affects all the men. The episode represents a distinct human experience.

Stewart wanders down the river fishing and sees Susan's body caught in the rocks. Hesitantly, he wades out to it and turns it over saying 'Oh Jesus' repeatedly. He screams for the others to come as he drags the body to the bank. He is obviously upset, making the sign of the cross. Stewart tells Rocco to 'take her, for fuck's sake, take her' and their shock is obvious. They all stare at the body and Billy goes to run off but they stop him. The four men meet and decide to leave her in the water and tie her so she doesn't float away.

The presence of the body threatens to detract from the enjoyment of the fishing experience. The act of attempted isolation of the bad experience is expected to evoke only a mild response. They do not anticipate the stormy reaction it receives when they return to the community.

The men go on fishing, with Stewart getting the first big fish on an absolutely perfect day. The lure of the fish is strong, especially when they see the big one he has caught. They have a successful and enjoyable time, a positive experience. They get a photo of the catch and Billy holds up his fish in a typical hunter/gatherer pose. Capturing an experience this way is most enjoyable.

It is a photo that will come back to haunt them as things change back in the world. An unanticipated adverse reaction can be a horrific experience.

Stewart goes to check on the dead girl, rolling her over and getting debris off her face in a quite tender gesture. The next day they head back and report it. At the car Billy rings Elissa and says they found a body but 'caught the most amazing fish'. They are told by the police to wait and seem despondent their trip has been ruined. They organise their story as Stewart says they have 'to get their story straight'.

We cut to Gregory eating breakfast and he appears to be a normal, lonely man until he goes out to his shed where he has hidden Susan's car and this reminds us of the evil in him. Consider his experience and his motivations. How does he see his actions and the world?

The next day at the station the policeman tells the fishermen 'we don't step over bodies for our recreational pursuits' and 'the whole town's ashamed of you'. When they are told to 'piss off' from the station the press are waiting for them and Billy makes a comment. Carl is angry with the press but we can begin to see signs of distress within the whole group.

The experience they had so looked forward to has become a negative one and the tensions we saw before are exacerbated by the emotional and collective response to the murder. Claire soon becomes obsessed with the whole affair because of her own state. The newspaper the next day has the headline, 'Men fish over dead body' because Billy has talked. Billy is late to work and Stewart tells him they have to 'stick together on this'.

Susan's sister calls them 'animals' and raises the race question by asking if they would have left a white girl. The Aboriginal youths begin to attack and vandalise the property of the men in violent outbursts, including throwing a rock through Billy's van window and thus endangering his baby. They insult Carl at the caravan park and vandalise the garage.

The police aren't any help and the situation deteriorates. Jude tells the police they shouldn't be enforcing the 'political correctness' laws. The intervention of the sense of Aboriginality and race challenges the assumptions people have and how we see the world. The contrasting views are ingrained in the social structures and part of different collective experiences.

The Aboriginal people see the white people as 'interfering' and the group of fishermen begin to fight amongst themselves. Elissa says they shouldn't go to the bush at all as it's sacred. The group talk about the bush and Rocco punches Stewart for saying the Aborigines are superstitious. The experience of racial tension becomes ever-present and adds to the emotional responses to the experience.

We now head slowly to a resolution of the conflict brought about by the various experiences. Each is handled in a different manner by characters and you can explore one or two of the responses. To cycle back to the original murder, Claire is stalked by Gregory in his truck. He stops her but drives off after staring weirdly, an odd experience in itself.

Terry and Stewart talk and Stewart meets Rocco and Carl. He tells them Claire's left him 'again'. Rocco can't believe it and we cross cut to her looking out into the wilderness after he looks thoughtfully out the window. These different reactions to experiences mirror attitudes in life and reactions to emotional and intellectual conflict.

In conclusion, Lawrence takes us back to the healing power of nature in our human experiences when the Aboriginal people are having a ceremony. Gregory watches while Claire walks in. Again we see his truck as an omnipresent force in the film, almost an extension of him. An Aboriginal man tells Claire to 'piss off' from the ceremony after she says she has come to pay her 'respects' but he is told to leave her alone by an Auntie.

The smoke and tribal music symbolise the ceremonial nature of the setting and the camera pans around the scene and the bush. We see parts of the ceremony with chanting and clapping sticks. The camera moves in and out while other shots pan around the bush, giving us the full experience and Lawrence portrays this as a positive, healing experience.

Eventually Stewart, Tom, Carl, Jude and Rocco arrive to pay respects. Tom runs to his mother and Stewart goes over and says 'Sorry' but is rebuffed by the father who throws dirt on him and spits, refusing his apology. Then an Aboriginal girl tells a little about Susan's story and sings the last love song Susan wrote.

The camera pans around all the faces as they listen to the song and the ceremonial smoke wafts around. It seems to have some healing effect on everyone, as it is a meaningful experience which raises the idea of the spiritual experience in the text. The girl stops singing through emotion. 'Be gone' seems to symbolise in language the whole scenario for each character.

We see a long wide shot of the bush before fading back to Gregory waiting again in his car behind the rocks for another victim. It is quite a circular conclusion and it is an odd end when he crushes the fly. We don't quite know what to make of the whole experience and he seems to be the only character unchanged by the experiences in the film.

Poem: 'Inland' by John Kinsella

The poem captures the mood and ethos of the outback farming communities and deals with the human aspect more than some of the other poems in Kinsella's collection: *Peripheral Light*. This poem is one long restless thought that mimics memories and recollection while raising the current, topical issues that concern the poet. As usual with his poems Kinsella orientates the audience early with the word 'Inland' and then continues the poem without a full stop. The poem flows with the use of commas but Kinsella allows us to stop and think with the use of the colon, brackets and the hyphen. Look for these punctuation stops as you read as they emphasise a specific point or idea that resonates with the audience.

The first stanza gives us a foreshadowing of the events to follow with the warnings in the words 'storm', 'alert' and 'uncertain'. This ominous tone is reinforced by the word 'ghosts' and the implication of death which is constant in much of Kinsella's poetry. The next stanza deals with a more human element and we get the country feel with the bracketed gossip about McHenry's accident which shows the close knit community. Habits here are formed as part of survival and known to all as we see 'the old man plying the same track' and the families possibly heading to church on the Sunday morning.

The third stanza returns to the vagaries of nature. Kinsella repeats 'uncertain' with regard to the weather. Weather and the environment play a large role in farming communities and it is especially so at sowing and harvest. Despite the uncertainty and 'ashen' days which alter 'moods', the community returns to their habits and routines which shape their lives. The next stage returns to the road and the implication of a journey but a journey that is straight and in conflict with the cycles of the natural world. The path seems already marked and measured. It is 'straight and narrow', marked by a theodolite.

The final four lines of the poem are pure Kinsella, marking the transience of humanity on the landscape. We read

> 'it's a place of borrowed dreams
> where the marks of the spirit
> have been erased by dust –
> the restless topsoil'

The European farmers had 'borrowed dreams' for their own relationship with the land but this line also harks back to the indigenous Dreamtime when the land was created. The indigenous view that the land owns the people is also true for Kinsella. This sense of nobody owning the land is strong in his poetry. European impact on the land can be seen in the spirituality being removed by the dust—dust created by the poor farming techniques transferred from a different land. He finishes with the 'restless topsoil' as if the whole earth is moving in its own discontented journey, just as the people move.

The influence here of genuinely lost spirituality and connection with the land as we move directly on the 'high road' contrasts with the more flowing, 'restless' side of the natural world. This visual contrast is obvious but we can also discuss the contrast between habit and spirit. 'Inland' is a poem that uses the landscape to show the contrast between two views of the countryside.

DRAMA: Eugene O'Neil's *Desire Under the Elms*

O'Neill sets out to instruct how the house and elms should appear and the year is 1850. Note how he describes the 'enormous' elms as,

> 'exhausted women resting their sagging breasts and hands and hair on its roof, and when it rains their tears trickle down monotonously and rot on the shingles'

and how they dominate and 'rot'. It is important to read this both in terms of the play and in the context of American theatre. The description here shows O'Neill's genius at new design and original theatricality.

Part One: Scene One

The whole first page and a third are nearly all playwright notes that describe the farm, the house and the characters of Eben, Simeon and Peter. The first words of the play, 'God! Purty!' reflect the beauty of the land and how Eben perceives it. Eben is 'resentful and defensive' and feels 'trapped' on the farm.

His older half-brothers Simeon and Peter are 'more bounce and homelier in face, shrewder and more practical.' They all have worked hard on their father's farm over the years and have little feeling for their absent father. We learn that Simeon had a 'woman' who died and that Peter is excited by the prospect of 'gold in the West'. They all talk about how hard they've worked and hope that the father might 'die soon'. What we get from all this is that they are earthy and this is reflected in their bodies and clothes which are all dirt stained.

We also see here the difference between them as Eben sees gold in the pasture, not California, as they head in for a dinner of bacon in what seems a ritual they have performed many times before. Note that O'Neill calls for the use of the curtain at the end of the scene.

Scene Two

It is twilight and again we get detailed notes on the interior scene. Simeon tells Eben he should not wish their father dead and Eben replies he's not his son but, 'I'm Maw – every drop of blood!' He then blames the father, Ephraim Cabot, for killing his mother by working her to death but the others just say there was work to be done. O'Neill gets them to list the jobs and Eben comes back with 'vengeful passion' that, while they did nothing, he will see his mother gets 'rest and sleep in her grave!'

They then discuss Cabot's absence and how he just drove off in a buggy one day in a rush. Simeon says that when he went,

> 'He druv off in the buggy, all spick an' span, with the mare all breshed an' shiny, druv off clackin' his tongue an' wavin' his whip. I remember it quite well'

Eben mocks Simeon for not stopping him and the scene concludes with Eben leaving to see Minnie the town whore. We learn all the Cabot men have slept with her. Simeon and Peter say that Eben is just like 'Paw' and thinks of California. The final image is of Eben with his arms stretched to the sky talking about starts and sin, 'my sin's as purty as any one on 'em!', until he 'strides' to the village for Min.

Scene Three

It is 'pitch darkness' and Eben comes home with the news that Cabot has married a 'purty' thirty-five year old. He has heard this in the village and this effectively disinherits the boys. Simeon and Peter see California as their only option now. Eben tells the boys that they can have three hundred dollars each if they sign their share of the farm over to him. He can get the money as his mother told him,

> 'I know whar it's hid. I been waitin' – Maw told me. She knew whar it lay fur years, but she was waitin'....It's her'n – the money he hoarded from her farm an' hid from Maw. It's my money by rights now.'

They think about it and Eben tells them about his night with Min. He tells how he hates the new wife after the boys suggest he might sleep with her, just like Min, to get the old man back. Peter and Simeon say they'll do the deal and leave the farm. Both are bitter and vindictive about Cabot.

Scene Four

The setting is the same as Scene Two and the boys are discussing how they don't have to work now – it is all down to Eben who is jubilant as he thinks it will all be his. Peter and Simeon again reflect on how like his father he is, 'Like his Paw'. They also tell he isn't much of a milker but they soon talk about their leaving and how they'll miss some aspects of the farm.

Eben comes back in and says that the 'old mule an the bride' are coming. The two older boys begin to pack and sign Eben's papers as he gives them the money Cabot had hidden. They tell him they'll send him 'a lump o' gold for Christmas' and head into the yard feeling 'light' because of their newfound freedom.

Ephraim Cabot and Abbie Putnam then come in and O'Neill describes them in detail. Cabot is

> 'seventy-five, tall and gaunt, with great, wiry, concentrated power, but stoop shouldered by toil. His face is hard as if it were hewn from a boulder, yet there is a weakness in it'

but his face is weakened with petty pride. Abbie is

> 'thirty-five, buxom, full of vitality. Her round face is pretty but marred by its rather gross sensuality. There is strength and obstinacy in her jaw, a hard determination in her eyes, and about her whole personality.'

She also has a 'desperate quality'. Cabot shows Abbie the place and she says to him it's 'mine'. Then he sees the two boys not working. He introduces Abbie and she goes to look at 'her' house and they warn her Eben's inside.

Cabot tells them to get to work and they give him cheek, saying they are 'free' and heading to California. They 'whoop' it up and he says he'll have them chained up. They throw rocks at the house, smashing the window and head off singing. Abbie sticks her head out the window and says she likes the room but he is thinking of the stock and 'almost runs' to the barn.

Abbie then meets Eben in the kitchen and talks to him in 'seductive tones'. She says she doesn't want to be his 'Maw' but friends and he cusses her. She tells him of her troubled life and how Cabot gave her a chance to escape it. He calls her a 'harlot' and they argue over ownership of the farm. She has the upper hand in law and he leaves but the seeds of their growing attraction have been set.

Outside he and his father argue about life and work and he tells Eben 'Ye'll never be more'n half a man!' The scene ends with Abbie washing up and the faint notes of the song the boys were singing as they left.

Part Two: Scene One

Again O'Neill describes in detail the farmhouse setting. Two months have passed and it is a hot Sunday afternoon. Abbie in her best outfit is sitting on the porch and Eben comes out of the house also dressed in his best. They stalk each other, both attracted and repelled. As he walks away she 'gives a sneering, taunting chuckle' at him and they argue but the attraction is obvious. She says that nature will pull him to her but he says that she is married and he goes to leave her.

She accuses him of going to Min and she gets angry stating he'll never get the farm,

> 'Ye'll never live t' see the day when even a stinkin' weed on it 'll belong t' ye!'

He says he hates her and leaves as Cabot enters. She tells him Eben has been mocking him and twists the conversation to the inheritance of the farm. She tells him Eben lusts after her and as he angers she backs off in her accusations. Reassured, he says that she can have the farm if she bears the son she says she wants with him. He says that he'd 'do anythin' ye axed, I tell ye!' if she gave him a son and tells her to pray to God for it to happen.

Scene Two

It is about eight in the evening and here the bedrooms are highlighted, with Eben in one and Cabot with Abbie in the other. The two of them are talking about a son. They seem together, yet apart, as he tells her of his life on the farm and how God's hard. He both lost and gained on the way through, but the farm is his. He says he is pleased he found her, his 'Rose o' Sharon'. Abbie promises him that she will bear a son as he basically threatens her,

> 'Ye don't know nothin' – nor never will. If ye don't hev a son t' redeem ye...'

and he leaves to sleep in the barn with the cows 'whar it's restful'.

We then see Eben and Abbie restless and she leaves the room and goes to him. He 'submits' to her kisses then 'hurls' her away. Abbie says she'd make him 'happy' and she knows he wants her too much. She tells him to go down to the parlour and he is shocked as this is where his mother was 'laid out'. She leaves for the parlour and he wonders what's happening. The scene closes with a question to his dead mother, 'Maw! Whar are yew?' but we know that he wants her and will go to her.

Scene Three

The scene now shifts to the parlour which is described as a 'grim, repressed room like a tomb'. Abbie waits and Eben appears and he sits at her invitation. They talk about his Maw and how they hate Cabot. Abbie throws herself at him with 'wild passion' and he is caught up in the moment and thinks that it's his Maw wanting him to sleep with Abbie to get revenge on Cabot,

I see it! I sees why. It's her vengeance on him – so's she kin rest quiet in her grave!

Abbie proclaims her love for him and he for her then they kiss 'in a fierce, bruising kiss' to close the scene.

Scene Four

A more bold and confident Eben leaves the house and Abbie opens the parlour window. She calls him over for a kiss and they talk a bit before Eben says his Maw can now rest. They split as Cabot comes out of the barn but are now obviously in love. Eben tells Cabot that his Maw is now at rest and Cabot says he rests best with the cows. Cabot is confused but the scene ends with him criticising Eben as 'Soft-headed' and a 'born fool' but, being a practical man, he heads for breakfast.

Part Three: Scene One

Time has passed to 'late spring the following year'. Eben is upstairs in emotional and psychological conflict while a party happens downstairs. Cabot has drunk too much and Abbie sits, pale and thin, in a rocking chair. There is a fiddler and Abbie begins the scene by asking for Eben and the guests 'titter' as most think the baby is Eben's, not Cabot's, which is true enough. They laugh and Cabot is angered by this and orders them to dance. The fiddler 'slyly' says they're waiting for Eben but Cabot mocks the boy and then ensues a bawdy conversation about his fertility,

> I got a lot in me – a hell of a lot – folks don't know on.
> Fiddle 'er up, durn ye! Give 'em somethin' t' dance t!'

The fiddler plays and they dance. Cabot joins in frantically and 'whoop(s)' it up. He exhausts the fiddler and pours whiskey. In the upstairs room Eben is looking at the baby. Abbie goes upstairs and Cabot leaves for outside, 'fresh air', as she has told him not to 'tech' her. The guests gossip after he goes and we see Eben and Abbie upstairs and she professes her love for him,

> 'Don't git feelin' low. I love ye, Eben. Kiss me.'

Cabot says he's going to rest in the barn. The scene concludes with the fiddler playing in celebration of 'the old skunk gittin' fooled!'

Scene Two

Eben is outside half an hour later and Cabot is coming back from the barn. Cabot tells him to get a woman inside and he might get a farm. Eben replies that this farm's his and Cabot mocks him. He tells her Abbie has been promised the farm for her son and Eben is angered thinking Abbie has tricked him.

Eben goes to kill her but Cabot is too strong for him and Abbie comes out to stop him choking Eben. Cabot tells him he's weak and goes inside to celebrate. Abbie tries to be tender with Eben but he rejects her and calls her a liar.

> 'Ye're nothin' but a stinkin' passel o' lies. Ye've been lyin'
> t' me every word ye spoke, day an' night, since we fust –
> done it. Ye've kept sayin' ye loved me....'

She says she loves him and tells him that the promise was made before they fell in love. He says he'll go to California.

They argue and he 'torturedly' says he wished the baby had never been born. Abbie is distraught and she says she'd kill the baby to prove her love for him. He says he won't listen to her but she calls after him that she can 'prove' she loves him and she 'kin do one thin' God does'. Abbie is desperate at the end of the scene.

Scene Three

It is now just before dawn and Eben is in the kitchen ready to leave. Abbie is near the cradle with 'her face full of terror'. She sobs but Cabot stirs and she goes to the kitchen and flings her arms around Eben, kissing him 'wildly'. She says 'I killed him' and he thinks she means Cabot but is horrified when she tells him it's the baby.

Eben states it was his baby and she says she loved it but loves him more. He is angered,

> 'Don't ye tech me! Ye're pizzen! How could ye – t' murder
> a pore little critter – Ye must've swapped yer soul t' hell!

and tells her that he is getting the Sheriff and heads, 'panting and sobbing' to town. She calls out to him that she loves him.

Scene Four

It is after dawn and Abbie is in the kitchen. Cabot wakes in his room and is concerned that he has woken late. He checks the baby and is proud it is quiet and asleep. He goes down to Abbie in the kitchen and she tells him the baby is dead. He runs to check and comes back down and asks 'why?'

In a rage she tells him it was Eben's son and that she loves Eben, not him. He blinks back a tear and then gets 'stony' so he can carry on and says he is going to get the Sheriff. Abbie tells him that Eben's already gone so that Cabot tells her he'll 'git t' wuk.' He then tells her he'd never have told and now he's going to be 'lonesomer'n ever!' Eben comes back and Cabot tells him to get off the farm.

Eben asks for her forgiveness and tells her he loves her. He says he realised he loved her at the Sheriff's and they have a chance to run away but Abbie says she'll take her punishment. Eben says he will share it with her and plans to tell the Sheriff they planned it together. They think they can stand it together and then Cabot comes back.

He goes into a long tirade and tells them how he's let the stock go and will burn the house down. He too plans to go to California but finds that Eben has gotten to his money first. Cabot says that this is a sign from God to him to stay and that 'God's hard an' lonesome!' At this point the Sheriff comes and Eben says he was involved with the baby's murder.

Cabot says 'Take 'em both' and leaves to get his stock. The sun is coming up and as they are led away Eben says the farm's 'Purty' and Abbie agrees. The Sheriff finishes the play with the line, 'It's a jim-dandy farm, no denyin'. Wish I owned it!'

OTHER RELATED TEXTS

Fiction / Non-fiction / Drama

- *Wonder* – R G Palacio
- *First they Killed My Father* – Luong Ung
- *The Graveyard Book* – Neil Gaiman
- *Looking for Alaska* – John Green
- *Eleanor and Park* by Rainbow Rowell
- *The Fault in Our Stars* – John Green
- *We All Fall Down* – Robert Cormier
- *The Old Man and the Sea* – Ernest Hemingway
- *The Fire Eaters* – David Almond
- *Ender's Game* – Orson Scott Card
- *Hatchet* – Gary Paulsen
- *Inside Black Australia* – Kevin Gilbert
- *Sapiens: A Brief History of Humankind* – Yuval Noah Harari
- *Peeling the Onion* – Wendy Orr
- *Raw* – Scott Monk
- *Six Degrees of Separation* – John Guare
- *The Book Thief* – Markus Zusak
- *When Dogs Cry* – Markus Zusak
- *Holes* – Louis Sachar
- *The Outsiders* – S.E. Hinton
- *Roll of Thunder, Hear My Cry* – Mildred D. Taylor
- *A Small Free Kiss in the Dark* – Glenda Millard
- *Monster* – Walter Dean Myers
- *Lord of the Flies* – William Golding
- *Jandamarra* – Steve Hawke
- *A Separate Peace* – John Knowles
- *A Monster Calls* – Patrick Ness
- *The Pigman* – Paul Zindel
- *The Invention of Hugo Cabret* – Brian Selznik

- *Emerald City* – David Williamson
- *Silent Spring* – Rachel Carson

Films and Television

- *The Human Experience* – Charles Kinnane
- *My Brilliant Career* – Gillian Armstrong
- *Broadchurch* – James Strong & Euros Lyn
- *Twinsters* – Samantha Futerman and Ryan Miyamoto
- *Be My Brother* – Genevieve Clay - Smith
- *What's Eating Gilbert Grape* – Lasse Hallstrom
- *Pleasantville* – Gary Ross
- *Eternal Sunshine of the Spotless Mind* – Michel Gondry
- *Taxi Driver* – Martin Scorsese
- *Tootsie* – Sydney Pollack
- *Back in Time for Dinner* – Kim Maddever
- *The Godfather* – Francis Ford Coppola
- *Friends* – David Crane and Marta Kaufmann
- *Dawson's Creek* – Kevin Williamson
- *Orange is the New Black* – Jenji Kohan
- *Boy Meets World* – Michael Jacobs and April Kelly

Website – quote on literature and the human experience

*http://view2.fdu.edu/academics/university-college/school-of-humanities/
english-language-and-literature-program/*

> At its most fundamental level literature explores what
> it means to be a human being in this world and tries
> to describe what our human experience is like. As
> such, literature pushes us to confront the large human
> questions that have plagued humankind for centuries:
> issues of fate and free will, issues relating to our
> role in the universe, our relationship to God, and our

relationships with others. Studying literature not only helps us to understand the complexity of these questions intellectually, but because of its very nature, it allows us to experience these tensions vicariously. Literature does not just tell us about human experience; it recreates it in a way we can feel and visualise. In other words, it calls for a total response from us—it stretches us beyond who we are.

First, literature can enhance our ability to relate to people. Because literature focuses on human relationships and self perception, it can broaden our own experience—to help us understand different kinds of people, different cultures, different problems—and, consequently, help us better understand our own relationships with others.

The study of literature also helps to foster an appreciation for beauty, symmetry, and order. This means more than the intuitive response of liking or disliking something we see or read or hear; it means a carefully thought-through response that will enhance appreciation—not destroy it.

Perhaps the most important skills that the study of literature teaches are analytic and synthetic skills. In learning to read carefully and analytically, we learn to ask hard questions both of the work and of ourselves. And as we seek to discover the relationships between the ideas and images we uncover in a work, our ultimate goal is to see the whole—to see how the parts work together to make the piece what it is. In grappling with the complex and difficult ideas contained in literature, we learn to accept the multiple dimensions and ambiguity that are so often present in life.

Finally, the study of literature will also help develop our writing abilities as we come to value the written word and understand its power to communicate.

Beyond all of these skills, however, it is not what literature can do for us as individuals as much as what it can do to us. Literature speaks to the whole person. Listen to it, says C. S. Lewis, and you will be changed.

Poetry

- 'Warren Pryor' – Alden Nowlan
- 'The Gardener' – Louis MacNeice
- 'The Improvers' – Colin Thiele

Songs

- *Be My Escape* – Relient K
- *Mandolin Wind* – Rod Stewart
- *Roxanne* – The Police
- *Wake Me Up When September Ends* – Green Day
- *Under Pressure* – Queen & David Bowie
- *Candle in the Wind* – Elton John
- *Empire State of Mind* – Alicia Keys
- *Gold Digger* – Kanye West
- *We Are Young* – Fun.
- *Centrefold* – J. Geils Band
- *It's Time* – Imagine Dragons
- *We Cry* – The Script
- *If I Were a Boy* – Beyoncé
- *Shake it Out* – Florence + the Machine
- *C'mon* – Panic! At the Disco & Fun.
- *I Don't Love You* – My Chemical Romance
- *Sing* – My Chemical Romance
- *1985* – Bowling for Soup
- *What About Me* – Shannon Noll
- *Sinner* – Jeremy Loops
- *7 Years* – Lucas Graham

- *Bitter Sweet Symphony* – The Verve
- *Ghost!* – Kid Kudi
- *Good Riddance (Time of Your Life)* – Green Day
- *Expectations* – Belle and Sebastian
- *After Hours* – We Are Scientists
- *Write About Love* – Belle and Sebastian
- *Trust Your Stomach* – Marching Band
- *Heaven Knows I'm Miserable Now* – The Smiths